1/500
Feb

CHILDREN'S
WEAR
DESIGN

CHILDREN'S WEAR DESIGN

BY *HILDE JAFFE*

Illustrated by ROSEMARY TORRE

FAIRCHILD PUBLICATIONS, INC.

New York

Standard Book Number: 87005-099-0
Library of Congress Catalog Card Number: 77-180154

Printed in the United States of America
DESIGNED BY VINCENT TORRE

PHOTO CREDITS: Coxe Photograph, p. 27; Henry Elrod Photography, p. 36;
Courtesy of C. Schneider International Corp., p. 72; Reprinted from *Machine Made
Laces* by Coleman Schneider, p. 67; Photos by Lee White, pp. 91, 92, 94, 95, 96, 97,
98, 99, 100, 103, 104; *Women's Wear Daily* Photo, 35.

Contents

PART I
Background Information

PART II
Creative Patternmaking

Illustrations

Foreword

At last, the Children's Wear Industry has been put down on paper! The need for such a book has been long overdue!

A student of Children's Wear may greatly benefit by all the information gathered here, which otherwise could take years of experience to acquire.

All the principles of good design—proper fabrics, fit, trim etc.—to make "Childhood a very special time," are found between these covers.

Hilde Jaffe's book will perform a great service to our industry—and to the young who will benefit from it in the future.

Betsy Daniels
Designer, Shutter Bug
3/2/72

Foreword

Teacher, Designer, Colleague, Friend: Mrs. Jaffe has dared to write a "first;" a book clearly presenting the basics of creating original designs, complete for all ages and stages of childhood from newborn to teenager. "Children's Wear Design," a book as exciting as New York City, covering all aspects of interest to the student, is well written, superb in detail, instructions easy to understand and follow—and a profusion of well selected illustrations and diagrams. Her methods are flawless, step by step, and thoroughly researched to assure results, yet are phrased to avoid the too-technical approach of many texts in design.

While this book is particularly useful as a primary text for the student designer, it has other appeal. It is also a most useful book for those who are studying the broader area of children's clothing; that it provides insight for the consumer as well as the designer; especially with the inclusion of a fine section on the child, his needs and activities. Educators seeking a critical survey of all aspects of children's clothing will find this book invaluable, and may serve to give ideas and content for courses in this area.

I am pleased to write this foreword for Mrs. Jaffe's stimulating manuscript. A few weeks ago Mrs. Jaffe phoned me to tell me she had written "The Book." When there was no immediate reaction on my part, she reminded me of a time when she had told me about her work at F.I.T. and I said "why don't you write a book?"

Mrs. Jaffe is eminently qualified to author "Children's Wear Design." She has been a successful designer for many years, is now an associate professor, teaching design and related courses. Having taken work at Queens College, she is remembered by her professors as a very able person. Her book indicates this; is authoritative, aimed to inspire performance and creativity. The prime ingredient is excellence.

Margaret A. Gram
Professor and Chairman of the
Department of Home Economics
Queens College
March, 1972

Preface

Designing children's wear requires a certain amount of background knowledge and various technical skills along with the intangible, but essential, creative talent that the aspiring designer must have to begin with. The purpose of this book is to provide the special information needed by the children's wear designer to function effectively on a professional level.

The first part of the text explores the various areas that form the framework by which children's wear design is limited. Limitations imposed by size ranges, textiles, and production methods are analyzed. A rudimentary outline of the physical and mental growth of children is presented with emphasis on children's clothing requirements at each developmental stage. Since understanding the needs and the growth of children is most important for the designer, I hope that the sketchy information presented here will serve as motivation for continued interest and further study in this area. The brief look into the history of children's apparel manufacturing should help the designer see her work in the context of a continuously evolving industry that has emerged from the small, individually owned shop into "big business." Finally, I have attempted to show the new designer where inspiration can be found for the fresh, saleable ideas that must appear in every collection to impress the buyers and make the season a financial success.

Since wearable, well-proportioned children's apparel is dependent on the designer's ability to express her ideas in fabrics, emphasis throughout the second part has been placed on creative patternmaking. Although patterns can be made both by draping and drafting, the usual practice in the children's wear industry is to work with the flat patternmaking method. I have found that both methods can be used to advantage. New foundation patterns can be draped much more quickly and accurately on the dress form, rather than by drafting them from measurements. Also, by draping directly in fabric, it is easier to develop new shapes and silhouettes. On the other hand, once a foundation pattern has been perfected, it is much more efficient to work out variations by flat patternmaking. Step-by-step instructions are given for each method as it is used to solve individual cutting problems. It is important to note that the problems selected are only those typical of children's wear. This is not a comprehensive patternmaking book, and the methods used may, at times, seem somewhat unorthodox to the traditional patternmaker of ladies' wear. These are, however, the quick and efficient methods for children's wear. Except where otherwise indicated, all patternmaking diagrams are based on the size 4 foundation pattern, reduced to one quarter of its original size.

In the second section of Part II, the special problems encountered by designers in particular areas of children's wear are explored. Since the problems inherent in designing children's dresses are covered in the section devoted to basic patternmaking, there was no need to treat this specialty separately. This, of course, does not deny its important existence in the children's wear industry. Although the book is primarily intended as a guide for young designers, the garment measurements for the various specialties and the body measurements in the appendix should also be useful for patternmakers and graders.

It is expected that the reader has had some previous experience in sketching, sewing, draping, and patternmaking before specializing in children's wear design. For the F.I.T. students who use this text, this will be no problem, since they do not usually enroll in the children's wear classes until their senior semester. By this time, they have acquired an excellent background in the basic skills of design. Others with some previous elementary training should also be able to use this book to learn the professional know-how of children's wear design.

Although both men and women are successfully designing children's wear today, the majority of our students are women. Therefore, for the sake of expedience, I shall refer to the designer as "she" throughout the book. I do hope that all the men will forgive me.

The need for a text in children's wear design has been evident since the introduction of Children's Wear as a course of study at the Fashion Institute of Technology. Nothing on a professional level had been published in this area. Children's wear designers were trained on the job, and the quality of the training depended on the manufacturer who was willing to hire the novice. At F.I.T. every effort has been made to establish a curriculum that is grounded on the best experience in industry. This text is in line with this practice. Where my own personal experience was deficient, other designers readily cooperated to supply the necessary expertise. Particular thanks are due to Barbara Palmer, of Pandora, for her help with the section on sweaters; Estelle Halpern, of Dive-ettes, for her help with swimsuit design; and Annette Feldman, of Immerman Corp., who not only assisted with sleepwear, but contributed a willing ear and friendly counsel throughout.

I would also like to express my appreciation to the experts who are not designers, but who read special chapters and let me benefit from their invaluable experience. Thanks are due to Walter Lilie, who read the chapter on production methods, and David Singer, who was particularly helpful with the chapter on fabrics.

To the many enthusiastic students who readily cooperated with the testing of the material in this book, I am deeply indebted. Jo Bidner, who tested the patternmaking without classroom instruction, and Miriam Freilich, who read several chapters, were particularly helpful in providing the student's point of view. Not only was the material tested in my own classes, but also in the classes of my colleagues at F.I.T., Mrs. Selma Rosen

Preface

and Mrs. Rosa Rosa. They were both unfailingly generous with constructive suggestions. Mrs. Rosa, the designer for Tidykins, teaches at F.I.T. in the evening and was most helpful since her concurrent roles as designer and teacher enabled her to see problems from both points of view. But most of all, appreciation is due to Mrs. Selma Rosen, who read and tested just about every chapter of the book, and whose astute criticism and constant encouragement were priceless.

HILDE JAFFE

August 1971

PART I

Background Information

Chapter 1 / *Size Ranges*

OST aspiring children's wear designers have a mental image of the child they are planning to dress. It is usually a bright and charming youngster of uncertain age, with the dimples of a baby, the unselfconscious grace of the four-year-old, and enough baby fat to give the body a delicious roundness. Of course, there are any number of delightful children who fit this picture. It is important, however, to become aware of what children really look like before attempting to clothe them. The infant is vastly different in appearance from the pre-schooler, and the youngster in kindergarten again goes through many changes in physical development before he becomes a teen-ager.

It then follows that a design which might be perfect for a two-year-old toddler will appear ridiculous on the ten-year-old schoolgirl. In addition, since garments for children should be functional, it becomes apparent as we acquaint ourselves with children at different stages of development that the same outfit does not suit children of all ages. Later we will explore at greater length the development of the child, and how the clothing he wears satisfies some of his essential needs. For the present, however, let us limit ourselves to the specific problems which the designer and manufacturer face in providing clothes to fit the child as he grows from birth to adolescence.

To solve the problem of fit, as the proportions of the child change over the years, the manufacturer has divided the clothing for children of various ages into SIZE RANGES. Each range consists of sizes for children of similar proportions. A child outgrows a particular size range and proceeds to the next one when his body proportions change. Sizes, by and large, are related to the age of the child. There are, however, great variations in body build and development so that it does not necessarily follow that a five-year-old always wears a size 5. Children may vary greatly in height and weight at any given age according to their genetic heritage, nutritional habits, and other environmental influences.

Let us now examine each size range and determine the distinguishing characteristics in each.

Infants or Babettes

The garments in this range are for the baby from birth to the time when he begins to walk alone, at about one year. In infancy, the child's head is large in proportion to the rest of his body. It is approximately one fourth of his entire body length. The infant grows at a rapid rate during his first year. Although the average newborn weighs about 7½ pounds and is 20 inches tall, he almost triples his weight, and his body length increases over one third by the time he is a year old. Because of this swift development, sizes for garments change quickly, and the dress or sweater which seemed much too large for the baby is often outgrown before it is tried on again.

The sizes in this range are: 3 months, 6 months, 9 months, 12 months, and 18 months; or Small, Medium, Large, and Extra Large. In preparing models for this size range, the designer usually works in size 12 months, and this is called the "sample size."

Toddlers

The Toddler size range fits the child after he has learned to walk, until he is about three years old. During this period, general growth is not as spectacular as during infancy, but the arms and legs develop considerably. The legs become straight, and strong enough to easily support the body weight, and the arms become comparatively longer. The head of the child grows slowly in relation to the rest of his body, and the toddler does not seem quite as top-heavy as the infant. The stance of the

young child is different from the posture of the adult. The spine seems to curve in, producing what is called a swayback, and the stomach almost always protrudes. This baby stance sometimes continues to adolescence but more often disappears during the early school years.

Toddler sizes are: 1T, 2T, 3T, and 4T. The "T" stands for toddler; it avoids confusion, for size 3 and size 4 appear again in the next size range. Size 4T is used primarily in boys' wear and sportswear, very rarely in dresses. Sample size is 2T, because it is typical of this range.

Children

This is the size range in which most designers love to work, for here we encounter the children who are still charmingly unselfconscious but old enough to be fashionable. These are the youngsters of pre-school age from about three to six years. Their physical growth continues at a gradual, steady pace during this period. The average five-year-old child weighs 42.8 pounds and is 43.6 inches tall. His body is beginning to assume adult proportions and his legs grow rapidly; his trunk develops more slowly; and the size of his head changes very little. There is as yet no indication of a waistline, and the baby stance is still strong.

Sizes are: 3, 4, 5, 6, and 6x. Size 6x is larger than size 6 and of the same proportion. This size is not called size 7 because the proportions of the size 7 in the next size range are radically different. Sample size is size 4.

Until this stage, both boys' and girls' wear are manufactured in the same size ranges, often by the same manufacturer. For the school-age child, however, size ranges and manufacturing techniques are different for boys' and girls' wear. Boys' wear assumes the same styling and production methods as men's wear and therefore steps out of our present discussion. From school age on, we shall limit our studies to clothing for girls.

Girls

This size range is for the grade-schooler, usually the child from seven to ten years old. Growth continues at a gradual pace, but there is now a difference in the general appearance of the child as much of the baby fat decreases and is replaced by muscle tissue. For many girls, this is an awkward age, the stage between baby appeal and the eventual blossoming of youthful beauty. There is a definite slimming and lengthening of the torso and limbs, but as yet none of the curves of adolescence.

Size Ranges

Sizes are: 7, 8, 10, 12, and 14. Size 14 is now often eliminated by dress manufacturers, because the changes in dietary habits have made the chubby, shapeless ten- or eleven-year-old almost non-existent, and by the time the girl is twelve years old, she usually prefers to wear clothes from the Sub-teen size range. Some of the large mail-order houses, on the other hand, have recently requested manufacturers to size some garments from size 7 through 16. New product standards, developed by the United States Department of Commerce, have supported this prac-

tice. Taking into consideration the proportional growth of the school-age girl, as determined by a survey conducted by the Department of Agriculture, new standard body measurements have been developed for sizes 7 to 16. (See Appendix, page 256.) When the size range is 7-12, the sample size is size 8; for 7-14 or 16, the sample size is size 10.

Sub-Teens

At early adolescence, the girl experiences a spurt of growth. The torso becomes elongated and a natural waistline becomes apparent. Gradual breast and hip development begins, and although many children have only outgrown size 10 in the girls' sizes at this time, size 12 or 14 does not fit the newly emerging figure. The child in question will more likely fit into a size 6 or 8 of the Sub-teen range. This size range has been developed to fit the girl at the intermediate stage between late childhood and early maturity.

The sizes are: 6, 8, 10, 12, and 14. Sample sizes vary. Some dress manufacturers use size 8, and others prefer size 10. Sportswear manufacturers usually use size 12 as their sample size.

Young Juniors

At about the time when the adolescent girl enters high school, her figure has developed to almost adult maturity, and she has outgrown Sub-teen sizes. Now she has a definite waistline, high rounded breasts, and slim shapely hips. Young Junior sizes fit the teen-ager in late adolescence.

The sizes are: 3, 5, 7, 9, 11, and 13. Sample sizes vary, but size 7 seems to be the most popular. This range is not always considered a part of the children's wear industry. Some junior as well as children's wear manufacturers produce a Young Junior line.

Chapter 2 / *Child Development and Clothing for Children*

HILDREN develop in many ways. Aside from the obvious physical growth, intellectual, emotional, and social development occur. What are some of the needs of children as they gradually grow to adulthood, and what is the role of clothing in their lives? For example, it is widely believed that clothing affects the social behavior of children—the assumption being that the boy who is dressed like a gentleman will behave like one; or, on the other hand, that the child who is unkempt and goes to school in torn dungarees and dirty sneakers is a potential candidate for juvenile delinquency. Others believe that children acquire a sense of security by being dressed in the same sort of clothing as the other children in their group. Obviously, when we see a group of girls going to school, all wearing similar outfits, this appears to be true. But how important is this really to the child? If it is a real need, when does it begin to manifest itself, and at what age does it cease to be important? The designer is vitally concerned with these and other questions, but so far there has been very little scientific research in this area.

This is rather surprising, for a child in our civilization wears some kind of body covering from birth on through the entire span of his existence. Child psychology, although it has made tremendous progress in recent years, has rarely concerned itself with the effect of clothing on the development of the child, and very little verified evidence has been established. Whereas some studies have been done concerning teen-agers and their clothing, the years from infancy to adolescence have been almost totally neglected. Nevertheless, by observation and use of the limited data available, it is possible to arrive at some conclusion concerning the early function of clothing as we outline the development of the child from infancy, to the age of the toddler, on to the pre-school years, through school age and adolescence.

The Infant

At birth, the child is completely helpless and dependent on the adults who surround him for survival. He sleeps most of the time, except when he is hungry or otherwise uncomfortable. Within his limited sphere of perception, hunger and the discomfort caused by wetness, cold, excessive warmth, or the weight of heavy or restrictive covering become extremely acute suffering if not soon alleviated by the person who cares for him. His skin is very tender and chafes easily. He is extremely sensitive to changes in temperature, for his adjustment mechanism in this area is as yet underdeveloped. His sense of touch, however, functions almost perfectly from birth: he withdraws from irritation or becomes restless and cries.

In view of the needs of the infant, his clothing should be lightweight, soft, warm, and washable. Synthetic fibers, although very practical in terms of washability and easy care, should be carefully tested for comfort in wearing. When selected for use in outerwear, there is usually no problem, but for garments touching the infant's skin, nylon and polyesters should be blended with cotton for increased absorbency. Since the infant grows at a very rapid rate, garments made of stretch fabrics will fit for a longer period of time. They also permit more freedom of movement, a factor which has been generally acknowledged to be advantageous for optimum development of the child. The bulk of the ever-present diaper must be considered for the infant, and easy accessibility for quick changes is essential. Plastic diaper plants should be carefully designed so that all edges which touch the baby's skin are soft and non-irritating.

A baby learns about his world by looking at, touching, smelling, tasting, and manipulating the objects he can see and reach. Since part of this learning process is exploring himself and the clothes he wears, it is an essential safety factor that all small, decorative details and buttons be either eliminated entirely or securely fastened to the infant's garments.

At this stage, the child is not aware of the design of his clothing as long as it is not a source of discomfort. Therefore styling features are planned to appeal to the purchaser of the garment rather than the wearer.

There are primarily two classifications of purchasers of infants' wear: the mother and the grandmother. Mother is attracted by the functional and practical attributes of the design. She is especially concerned with ease of maintenance: washability and no-iron features are of primary importance. On the other hand, grandmothers and other doting relatives look for the little luxury touches, such as exquisite embroidery, delicate colors, ruffles, laces, and painstaking hand finishing.

The Toddler

During the period of beginning mobility, when the baby learns to walk, he is generally referred to as a toddler. His world is expanding as he begins to know and recognize more of the people and objects surrounding him. It is a period of exploration and experiment. As he moves about, he wants to handle everything he sees. He begins to respond and speak to others. In his first attempts to feed himself, he is often clumsy, and invariably mealtime is followed by a general cleanup of baby and the entire feeding area. Nevertheless, his muscular control develops and soon he is ready for toilet training, a process which is usually accomplished when the child is two and a half years old. His interest in clothes seems to be confined to taking them off, which he does whenever he has a opportunity. Evidently he is happiest when dressed in as few garments as possible, and he needs maximum freedom of movement.

Clothes for the toddler should be comfortable and protective. Overalls, protecting the knees against falls, and knitted shirts seem to be the most popular garments for boys as well as girls. This is the time for training pants, and they should be large enough so that the child can pull them on and off easily and quickly by himself. Since children at this stage dislike restrictive and heavy clothing, it is particularly important that outerwear be designed of lightweight, warm fabrics. Washable, quilted nylon jackets and snowsuits are a perfect answer to this problem, for they are warm, waterproof, and almost weightless.

Now girls' wear begins to differ somewhat from boys' wear, as girls will wear dresses and little boys wear pants and shirts for parties and special occasions. Sometimes the difference between girls' and boys' wear is merely a choice of color, pink being reserved for girls, while other colors are used for both sexes.

The Pre-School Child

From three to six years, the child matures rapidly. Although physical growth does not proceed at the same rate as earlier, the child changes markedly in the proportion of his body. His legs become longer and stronger. He loses some of the baby fat, and, in general, becomes more graceful and adept in his movements. He learns to run, skip, and climb. He rides a tricycle and throws a ball. He eats with reasonable table manners and communicates verbally. He gradually learns to play with other children and values their companionship.

He becomes aware of his clothes as he realizes that they will bring him attention and approval from adults. New garments are particularly important, for adults will notice and make pleasant comments. To the child, his clothing appears to be an extension of the concept of self. Therefore it would seem that when boys and girls are dressed appropriately to their sex, they identify as future men and women, and they grow up feeling more comfortable with their role. This may or may not be desirable. Some parents may prefer to minimize sexual differences by dressing boys and girls in similar clothes, hoping that thus they are fostering the optimum development of the child as a human being without the limitations imposed by sex roles.

Children at this age gradually learn to dress themselves and by the time they are four to five years old manage to do so quite efficiently as long as the clothing is easy to handle and has no complicated fastenings. Gesell and his colleagues observed normal children at the Yale laboratory and arrived at the following developmental sequence:

DRESSING

15 months 1. Cooperates in dressing by extending arm or leg.
18 months 1. Can take off mittens, hat, and socks.
          2. Can unzip zippers.
          3. Tries to put on shoes.
24 months 1. Can remove shoes if laces are untied.
          2. Helps in getting dressed—finds large armholes and thrusts his arm into them.
          3. Helps pull up or push down panties.
          4. Washes hands and dries them, but does neither very well.
36 months 1. Greater interest and ability in undressing. May need some assistance with shirts and sweaters.
          2. Is able to unbutton all front and side buttons by pushing buttons through buttonholes.
          3. In dressing, does not know front from back. Apt to put pants on backwards, has difficulty in turning socks to get heels in back. Puts shoes on but may put them on wrong feet.
          4. Intent on lacing shoes, but usually laces them incorrectly.
          5. Washes and dries hands.
          6. Brushes teeth with supervision.
48 months 1. Is able to dress and undress himself with little assistance.

2. Distinguishes between front and back of clothes and puts them on correctly.
3. Washes and dries hands and face.
4. Brushes his teeth.

60 months 1. Undresses and dresses with care.
2. May be able to tie shoelaces (usually at six years)[1].

Aside from the obvious benefits to mothers and nursery-school teachers, it is generally conceded that the child who is encouraged and manages to successfully dress himself at an early age will also act independently in other situations. Large armholes, back and front either alike or very easy to tell apart, front opening, and fasteners easy to manipulate are factors which make learning to dress an easier task for the child.

The child from three to six is very much aware of color. He prefers bright primary colors and red seems to be the favorite. Texture is also important to young children. They love the feel of fur and smooth soft fabrics. On the other hand, they often refuse to wear scratchy textures, such as some woolens and crisp organdy. The pre-schooler has not yet acquired the willingness to suffer for beauty or appearance.

In considering the desire to conform in dress to that of other children, most authors agree with Mary Ryan Shaw when she states, "Unlike the older child, the pre-school child is usually not interested in whether or not his clothing conforms to the type that other children are wearing. He doesn't yet belong, or wish to belong, to a peer group and so is not interested in factors which make him conform to the group." [2]

To test the above supposition, 60 children from four to twelve years old were asked a series of questions weighing their desire to conform in dress against various factors which are generally deemed to be more important for the pre-school age group. There were 20 children four to six years old, 20 children seven to nine, and 20 children ten to twelve. The wish to conform was tested against the desire to wear a favorite color, a new garment, mother's preference, and general comfort. In the total evaluation, 31 percent of the four-to-six group gave replies indicating the desire to conform, in spite of all the other factors; 33 percent of the seven-to-nine group indicated desire to conform, and only 20 percent of the early adolescents answered in favor of conforming. We must remember that the alternative factors were valid, and that the actual wish to conform is probably much more evident when there is no opposing pressure. As a result of this study, we must assume that pre-schoolers also prefer to be dressed in the same styles as their friends. The desire to conform in dress begins in kindergarten and reaches its height in the early elementary grades, before it seems to decline in adolescence.

For the designer of children's wear there must be a totally different approach in designing for the pre-school child, as compared to younger children. In contrast to the toddler, the child from three to six is an individual who is aware of clothing and has quickly developed some very definite preferences and opinions. Unfortunately, the young child is rarely present when his clothing is purchased. Then he will often irritate his mother by refusing to wear a garment for no apparent reason. A little investigation usually reveals the cause of the refusal. Perhaps a scratchy seam, uncomfortable fit, or the fact that he doesn't like the color could be responsible for the dislike. Situations such as these could be avoided if the child were taken along for the purchase and permitted to try on the garment. Discomfort and poor fit, especially, could be identified before buying. Most pre-school children don't enjoy shopping and trying on clothes, but if a shopping afternoon could be made short and pleasant many purchasing mistakes would be avoided.

In summary, then, we must consider that pre-schoolers like bright colors, soft, interesting textures, basic comfort, clothing which is easy to get in and out of, and that which is similar to what the other children are wearing. On occasion, pre-schoolers like the old familiar garment for its sense of security, but almost all of them like new clothes for the admiration and attention they bring to the wearer.

Middle Childhood

When the child enters school, his world expands. Parents, who were until now the only major influence on the child, begin to share their position of authority with teachers and other children. In order to adjust to this expanded environment, the child will attempt to modify his behavior so that he will gain approval from parents, teachers, and peers—not necessarily in that order, much to the dismay of some parents. There is usually very little conflict between the demands of parents and teachers. Both are pleased with intellectual progress, good social manners, and neat appearance. Although some parents may regret the loss of pre-school cuteness as the child grows taller and more angular, this is not serious to the child and his peers. The demands of the peer group, however, are often more complex, and the child must try to fit in and gain acceptance. This acceptance is usually based on the skills and desirable characteristics the newcomer brings to the group, and lacking these, he may be quickly rejected. Rejection or disapproval of peers at this age can have a continued effect on the self-concept of the child lasting often into adolescence and adulthood.

In order to be accepted, most youngsters will strive to be as good as, but not too much better than, the other children in the group. This applies to school, sports, and play skills. Vigorous active play is universally enjoyed by the school-age child. These children practice for hours to throw a ball competently, skip rope, skate, ski, swim, and dive. When

economically feasible, the natural desire is supplemented by professional lessons, for modern parents want their children to become competent in all sorts of sports and social activities. Appropriate equipment and sports clothing are necessary items for the middle-class child's wardrobe, and swimsuits, skating skirts, ski suits, and tennis dresses find a ready market.

As has been previously mentioned, it becomes most important to conform in appearance to the other children at this age. The desire to conform has nothing to do with adult standards of beauty. Some children have been known to wish they had braces on their teeth, just because everybody else was wearing them. When an already insecure child is not dressed like the other children, the results can be devastating, as demonstrated by the following case history.

Priscilla was about fourteen when the climax of her difficulties was reached. From year to year she had become more stubborn and withdrawn. In school she sat with an air of complete detachment. Although of superior intelligence, her work was inadequate and often incomplete. She had few friends and participated in no social activity. Often she would give no reply to questions and would sit biting her nails and stare truculently at people.

Priscilla was a graceful and attractive child who, had she been dressed in becoming clothes, might have been unusually charming. She had a small, sensitive face, but usually she had a hard and hostile expression. She seemed completely inaccessible and nobody really understood her.

Priscilla's parents were essentially well meaning but completely lacked understanding. The father was a minister, the mother a former schoolteacher. Both parents were educated and conscientious in their approach to life. They were sensitive, had high standards of duties and obligations, considered good manners and proper behavior important, and devoted themselves unselfishly to the upbringing of their two children, in whom they tried to instill their principles.

In spite of all these virtues, these parents were damaging their daughter. Priscilla was a timid and fearful little girl who craved warmth and closeness which she never obtained, since both parents were rather distant. When, at two years of age, Priscilla had a little brother who, different from the family pattern, was a gay and jolly baby, delighting his parents and everyone else with his cuteness, Priscilla felt utterly rejected and withdrew into a shell.

There is no doubt that her mother gave her much reason to feel that the brother was preferred. For one thing, the mother lacked understanding to such a degree that, following her moral principles, she demanded that the defeated little daughter enjoy the baby as much as she did, and later share things with him and not be jealous.

The unhappiness in which Priscilla lived, feeling rejected and also condemned for her jealousy, was increased by her unhappy school experiences. Priscilla went to school feeling that all the other children were happy and loved. Her feeling of isolation was increased as she became aware of the awkwardness of her clothing. Her mother believed in practical, homemade dresses. Neither parent believed in vanities. Thus Priscilla always wore too large, bulky dresses which the other children sometimes ridiculed.

Sullenness and a negative, stubborn antagonism toward the whole world became the mask beneath which Priscilla hid her hurt feelings. Her work was poor, although her intelligence was high. She had no friends. Her parents felt completely bewildered and outraged at their daughter's behavior. They tried everything they could think of—they admonished, scolded, punished, but to no avail. At twelve, Priscilla was fairly embittered, withdrawn, lonely, and unhappy.[3]

Psychoanalytic writers often refer to middle childhood as the Latency Period. It is a time when children withdraw from the heterosexual play of pre-school age to spend their time almost exclusively with companions of their own sex. Research has revealed that this phenomenon is true only in our own culture. In more primitive societies, heterosexual behavior increases continuously during middle childhood. The fact that children of this age group prefer friends of their own sex may erroneously give the impression that interest in boys has ceased, whereas, in fact, below the surface there is much concern and speculation about the opposite sex.

Girls of school age find expression for this concern in their identification with their mothers or, as is frequently the case, with a glamorous TV or movie star. Sometimes the idol is a favorite teacher or an older sister. In any case, the tomboy begins to hide her aggressiveness when she realizes that to be feminine is considered more attractive. Baseball, mechanics, and science are left to the boys; clothes, cooking, music, and art become the interests of most girls. And clothes should look like those worn by the identification idol. This explains the preference of schoolgirls for miniature versions of "Junior" styling. Young design features, such as suspender skirts, smocked dresses, and puffed sleeves, if they are not currently used in adult fashion, are vehemently rejected by the schoolgirl as being too babyish. On the other hand, sheer stockings and shoes with heels a little too high, worn with a grown-up dress, are the nine- and ten-year-old girl's idea of a really smashing outfit. It is up to the designer to create clothing for the schoolgirl with just the right touch of sophistication to satisfy the need of the child to feel feminine and attractive, while at the same time remembering that the schoolgirl is still a growing child, and her clothing should be comfortable and practical for play as well as school activities.

The Adolescent

Adolescence is a period of disorganization and stress. There are rapid spurts of growth and development, on physical, emotional, and intellectual levels. High demands are made on youth by our society. The emphasis on academic excellence creates tremendous pressures on many young people. Vital decisions have to be made. There is the necessity of career choice as adult responsibilities loom ahead. Rapid changes in body structure are disturbing and bring about the need for sexual adjustment. Adult values are often contradictory, and the teen-ager must come to terms with them, eventually forging his own code of ethics. Mussen, Conger, and Kagan wrote ". . . the adolescent in our culture is vitally concerned with assessing his liabilities and assets, trying on various roles to see which fit him most comfortably." [4] In this way, by trial and error, the adolescent will eventually develop his adult identity, but until this goal is realized, there is usually much frustration and strain.

Competitive activities are encouraged. An adolescent is expected to perform at least as well as, but possibly better than, his peers. This emphasis on excellence becomes more and more pronounced as teen-agers

become aware that the prizes of prestigious schools, recognition from teachers and peers, and general popularity are the result of outstanding performance.

The concept of being a leader becomes, for the most part, a desirable goal. For the designer, this means that many girls now are willing and eager to stand out among others as the best dressed. However, it must not be assumed that a girl is willing to be radically different in the choice of her apparel: she merely wants to stand out to the extent of having chosen the most recent and attractive version of the accepted fashion of the current season.

Adolescents, especially the girls, are more concerned about their physical appearance than their intellectual or social characteristics. The majority, even pretty ones, wish that they could change themselves so that they could measure up more closely to the stereotyped ideal of their group. In the effort to camouflage shortcomings and enhance physical assets, clothes play an important role. Dressed in the current fashion of the peer group, the adolescent can favorably revise her self-image. Fashion gives the teen-ager a sense of belonging to an accepted standard of dress, a reassurance that she may anticipate recognition and approval from those who count.

Those who count are usually not the parents. Unlike younger children, teen-agers love to go shopping, but a shopping trip with mother can prove to be a disaster. Mother has her convictions of what is appropriate and good-looking for a young girl, but daughter has her own ideas of what is right and attractive for her way of life. Often these are legitimate differences, reflecting the diversity of taste between the older generation and the young sophisticates of today. But on the other hand, some adolescents use the shopping decision as a means of asserting their independence and will oppose mother no matter what her preferences may be. As a result, many parents let their teen-agers do their own shopping without supervision. Surprisingly, most of the young people are quite knowledgeable in their choices, and quickly learn to appreciate quality and value as well as style. Special magazines keep teen-agers informed about the latest fashions and ideas for young people. Many department and specialty stores now have charge accounts for teen-agers, and are finding the operation profitable. Departments catering to the young set are swinging with pop decor and rock music.

To successfully design for the adolescent girl, one must understand her need to stand apart from the older generation, so that she may develop her own identity. Therefore, her clothes must be different, reflecting the taste of her own age group. Her self-confidence is bolstered by approval from her friends. She needs the companionship of boys to convince herself that she is sexually attractive, and expects her clothing to enhance her appearance. She expects much, and shops endlessly until she gets what she wants, but she is an important customer and her expenditures are formidable. For the designer, it is a constantly exciting challenge to keep up with young fads and fancies within the framework of fashion and good taste.

Child Development and Clothing for Children

NOTES

[1] Gesell, Arnold. *The First Five Years of Life—A Guide to the Study of the Pre-School Child.* p. 248.

[2] Ryan, Mary Shaw. *Clothing, A Study in Human Behavior.* p. 216.

[3] Mussen, Paul Henry, Conger, John Janeway and Kagan, Jerome. *Child Development and Personality.* p. 394.

[4] *Ibid.* p. 507.

Chapter 3 / *The Industry*

Historical Beginning

THE manufacture of children's wear began somewhat later than the production of ladies' garments, toward the end of the Industrial Revolution. Until the later half of the nineteenth century all garments were either made in the home or by professional dressmakers who created fashions to order for the individual customer. Unless mother was a talented seamstress, children's garments were either pretty clumsy or relatively expensive. As late as Spring 1897, we find only three pages devoted to little girls' wear in the entire Sears Roebuck catalogue.[1] There were some infants' dresses and cloaks, and an assortment of jackets for children up to twelve years old. These garments did not seem to present too much of a fitting problem. Evidently, dresses and playclothes for children didn't have much mail-order business potential, or they were not available in sufficient volume.

Aprons were popularly used to safeguard the precious dresses against spills and usual mishaps of active children. There were party aprons and school aprons, tailored aprons and aprons lavishly embroidered or trimmed with lace. Aprons were fairly easy to sew, and it developed that aprons were among the first garments to be manufactured in volume outside the home. Louis Borgenicht, an immigrant from Galicia who tells his story in *The Happiest Man*, was one of the first to enter the children's apron-manufacturing business in the 1880's. At first his wife did the actual sewing and he peddled the finished garments from door to door. He found that the early aprons had one serious problem. It was difficult to fit them on the various children of his customers. He then measured children of different ages and arrived at a set of corresponding sizes. The often-unwilling subjects received a custom-made apron as a reward for standing still long enough to supply the vital statistics.

Louis Borgenicht decided to expand into the production of dresses. Recalling this period, he wrote, "From my study of the market, I knew that only three men were making children's dresses in 1890. One was an East Side tailor, near me, who made only to order, while the other two turned out an expensive product with which I had no desire at all compete. I wanted to make 'popular price' stuff—wash dresses, silks and woolens. It was my goal to produce dresses that the great mass of the people could afford, dresses that would—from the business angle—sell equally well to both large and small, city and country stores." [2] He made up his first line with his wife's help, and since there was no competition, he was an immediate success. The customers at this time were the early New York merchants along with many retail customers, who constantly came to the store-front factory to buy. Soon, aprons were abandoned altogether, because of the pressure from stores to make dresses. Borgenicht now provided employment for other immigrants, many of whom were relatives, recent arrivals from his own region in Central Europe.

Wholesale manufacturing was on its way. By the beginning of the twentieth century, there was a thriving children's wear industry, mostly located in lower Manhattan. Competitors were other immigrants from Eastern or Central Europe, some of whom had learned the rudiments of the business in the employ of Borgenicht. These were the years of the sweatshop. Labor was plentiful and cheap in New York, as wave after wave of immigrants arrived, all looking for employment. The men, having learned their trade in the old country, were skilled tailors, or readily trained as cutters, and the women, mostly expert seamstresses, manned the sewing machines.

After 1920, there was an impressive change in manufacturing. Competition was keen, and we see some of the characteristic pressures of the garment business developing as Borgenicht writes:

"In the old days there had been one fall and one spring line of samples made up, with minor improvements and changes now and then between times. Year in and year out children's dresses had retained approximately the same characteristics. After 1920, however, when the need for volume made novelty and style prerequisites overnight, the public—exerting its influence through the store buyers—became the capricious dictator of our field. Not that we objected to this. It was simply not what we were accustomed to.

We had to forget our old schedule of two sample lines a year. We had to put out five, six and sometimes seven. The days when buyers came in and bought for the entire season were over. Instead they bought for two weeks. . . . Gone also were the days when we could buy our own raw goods six months in advance. Someone might bring out a pattern that would take the market by storm and we would be left with a loft full of worthless stock." [3]

It was at this time that the old production methods, where each garment was completed by one skilled worker, were replaced by modern section work. Training of labor was simplified as each operator needed to develop only the skill necessary to complete one unit of work, such as setting collars, seaming the side seams, or making buttonholes. This speeded up production tremendously and provided a much more economical use of the available labor.

As the industry expanded and buyers became increasingly selective, the work of the designer became more and more important. Parents and children, even in small towns and rural areas across the country, were exposed to improved communications media, and the current fashion message found its way into almost every home. In the '30's, movies had a tremendous impact on the children's wear market. Every little girl wanted to look like Shirley Temple, and stage-struck mothers encouraged tap-dancing and singing lessons for their offspring in the hope of duplicating the glamorous Hollywood moppet. Shirley Temple dresses, produced by Rosenau of Philadelphia, were a fantastic success, and contributed to making this firm the largest producer of children's wear in the world, a position which it maintains to this day.

Present Day Set-up

There have been many changes in the children's wear industry over the years. As the industry expanded and grew more sophisticated, manufacturers gradually shifted their headquarters uptown, and the majority are now located in mid-Manhattan at the southern end of the garment center. The buildings located at 112 and 130 West 34th Street are almost

Her Majesty plant

exclusively utilized for showroom and office space by children's wear manufacturers. Other "children's wear buildings" are located at Broadway and at Eighth Avenue near 36th Street. Having the industry so concentrated enables the buyer to shop the children's wear market without wasting too much time traveling from one manufacturer to the other. Space in the mid-town area, however, is expensive. Many manufacturers use these prime locations for showroom and office space only. Others also locate design-room, patternmaking, grading, and the shipping departments here. The firms who use independent contractors for their sewing operation may also locate their cutting departments in mid-Manhattan.

Manufacturers who own their own plants concentrate all their production in one place. Plants for New York-based firms are located in many areas. Pennsylvania and southern New England have had children's wear plants for many years. More recently the southern states, the Carolinas, Georgia, and Alabama, have provided desirable locations for children's wear factories. These modern plants, many in rural and suburban settings, with large parking lots for employees, are spacious and airy; a far cry from the early sweatshop.

Many sewing plants are independently owned. The owners contract work from several non-competitive manufacturers, or they might have an arrangement to work for one manufacturer exclusively. Working for a number of manufacturers assures the contractor of steady work for his employees.

Seasonal Lines

The garment industry is a seasonal business. In children's wear, as in other areas of the industry, the designer has to produce several lines a year. Opening dates for each line depend on the type of firm. The following analysis can serve only as a rough guide, because buyers tend to change delivery dates to meet current marketing needs. Sometimes changes are effected industry-wide and others are limited to certain manufacturers. Most manufacturers are willing to adjust the timing of their lines to meet the needs of the retailers. Mail-order houses and large chain stores, such as Sears and J. C. Penney, will want to see a line two to three months before the department and specialty stores. Catalogues need time to be printed, and the large chains make use of long-range planning. Buyers for department and specialty stores prefer to work more closely to the delivery dates for each season, as business and fashion trends can more easily be accurately assessed on a short-term basis.

The major lines in the children's wear industry are Back to School, Holiday, Spring, and Summer. In February, the designer usually begins work on the Back to School line. By the end of the month, the catalogue houses and large chains have already placed initial orders, but the official opening is around May 15th. During the last two weeks in May, buyers flock to New York from all over the country to shop the various lines and place orders for early August delivery to their stores. This is the season for tailored fall dresses and separates, as well as jackets and coats for school wear. Fabrics used are mostly washable wool blends, corduroy, and cottons. The warm climate of early fall and generally mild temperatures of the southern part of the country require a good proportion of lightweight clothing in this collection. Even though infants and toddlers don't go back to school, fall lines are designed for their size ranges to coincide with the rest of the industry. Dress manufacturers usually include a small group of understated party dresses for early fall social occasions.

During the summer months, the designer is busy with the velveteens and sheer fabrics of the Holiday line. This is usually a smaller collection with a relatively short selling season. Orders are placed in August; merchandise is delivered in November; and if it isn't sold by Christmas, it is marked down in January. Although the season is short, this is often the line with which the designer has most of the fun. Here is the chance to create those imaginative designs for special party occasions. Many manufacturers are willing to experiment with more expensive fabrics at this time, for this is the season when price-resistance is somewhat relaxed. Children's apparel is a popular gift item, and the major emphasis has temporarily shifted from utility and value to fantasy and fashion.

In September, work is begun on the designing of the Spring line. The first showing of this collection usually takes place in November, and buyers place orders for January delivery. There must be fresh merchandise in the stores after the post-holiday clearance sales. These orders are usually small, but they give the manufacturer an indication of which numbers are going to sell, and there is usually much discarding and filling in until the Spring collection is in final form for the January showing. During the first two weeks of January, buyers place substantial orders for February-March delivery. This is the real Easter business. Spring merchandise is distinguished by light, bright colors. Wool blends are used for coats and suits. Many lines include ensembles, dresses with jackets or coats. For southern climates, most manufacturers include some sleeveless cottons in their lines. There should be a good balance of tailored and dressy styles.

The Summer line is designed in January and shown to buyers in late February for after-Easter delivery to the stores. For dress manufacturers, this is a very small line, and outerwear producers don't have any Summer collections at all. On the other hand, this is the most important season for manufacturers of sports and swimwear. After all, what do children wear during summer vacation? Many dress manufacturers shift to playsuits and separates at this time in order to maintain a volume of business.

Various Specialties

In a discussion of children's wear manufacturing and manufacturers, we must understand that the field is so vast that it would be impractical for any one company to produce all the items necessary for a child's wardrobe. The industry is therefore divided into many specialties. Some manufacturers produce garments only for a certain age group, such as Infants' Wear. Others produce a certain type of garment in various age groups. For example, a dress manufacturer may produce dresses in the 3-to-6x and the 7-to-14 size ranges. Another may be so specialized as to produce only Sub-teen sportswear. The present trend toward mergers in the industry tends to result in large conglomerate firms with many divisions, manufacturing a variety of different specialties. When this is the case, however, different designers are usually employed to design each particular line. Following is an outline of the many specialties in the children's wear industry:

A. Infants' Wear
   Layettes—shirts, wrappers, gowns, buntings, etc.
   Stretch coveralls
   Diaper pants
   Dresses and suits
   Outerwear—pram suits, coats
   Knitwear—sweaters and cardigans, booties and hats
   Separates—diaper sets, crawlers, cotton knit polo shirts
Although some Infants' Wear manufacturers produce most of the above items, others specialize only in a limited type of merchandise.
B. Toddler Wear for Boys and Girls
   Brother-and-sister sets—shorts, skirts, overalls, shirts, etc.
C. Sportswear
   Slacks and shorts
   Skirts and jumpers
   Blouses and shirts
   Jackets and vests
   Sweaters
   Swimsuits
D. Dresses
   Tailored and party dresses
   Ensembles
   Jumpers and blouses
E. Sleepwear and Lingerie
   Robes
   Pajamas and nightgowns

Slips and petticoats
Shirts and panties
Hosiery
F. Outerwear
   Coats
   Jackets and carcoats
   Ski and snow suits

The Manufacturing Process

To understand the organization of the industry as it affects the designer, it might be useful to trace the manufacture of a child's garment from its original idea to the finished product. Before the designer begins to work on a line, she usually selects the fabrics she will use for her collection. As salesmen from the various textile houses come to see her, she picks the patterns and textures that appeal to her and orders a sample cut of each. The sample cut is usually from three to six yards long, depending on the size range and type of garment for which the fabric is intended. Sometimes the fabric suggests an idea to the designer. At other times, the designer sketches the idea first and then finds suitable fabric. In any case, once the sketch is made and the fabric selected the first sample has to be cut. In contrast to the usual practice in other areas of the garment industry, most designers of children's wear make their own first patterns and cut their own samples. In recent years, however, the practice of having an assistant cut the first sample has been adopted by some of the larger manufacturers. This permits the designer to devote herself exclusively to the creative aspect of her work, and in most cases results in more efficient utilization of her talents. Other designers still prefer to cut their own samples, evolving changes as they go along. To them, draping and cutting are a part of the creative process.

Once the first garment is cut, the sample-maker takes over. She is an expert seamstress, and following the designer's sketch, she sews the sample. In some sample rooms, there are finishers who do hand-finishing, such as sewing hems and attaching buttons. Other sample rooms are equipped with special machines for these operations, and the sample is finished to look like the usual stock garment. A professional presser is employed for the final pressing and the sample is complete. Throughout this process the designer keeps a close watch as the sample takes shape, making changes or corrections as needed. Before being presented to the executives of the firm for approval, the sample is "draped" on a hanger. This process involves pinning up and stuffing with tissue paper so that the dress is

displayed to best advantage. This effort to create ultimate hanger appeal is very important, since children's wear is not shown on live models, as is the practice in the adult areas of the garment business.

When the first sample has been completed it is presented for adoption by the firm at what is usually scheduled as a weekly staff meeting. Among the executives who usually have to approve a first sample are the sales manager, the production man, the piece-goods buyer, and the owner of the firm, if he does not function in one of the already mentioned capacities. All usually have to agree that they like the sample's styling. At this time, the designer must point out the new trends in fashion and other sales features that have been incorporated in the design. Production and sales people are usually not as alert to new directions as the designers. The sales manager keeps in mind what appeal the garment will have in the various regions of the country. What will sell in New England in mid-winter might have no market value in Florida or Texas at the same time of the year. He considers the sample in terms of value. Will it sell at the market price it must get, in view of particular fabric and labor costs?

These manufacturing costs are analyzed in detail by the production man. To help him, the designer has supplied him with a cost sheet for every sample. He carefully figures the garment, taking into consideration the cost of fabric used, the cost of trimming and notions, and the cost of labor. Before the actual wholesale price is arrived at, a percentage is added to cover general overhead expenses and to provide for profit. If the garment does not figure into the usual price range of the particular manufacturer, it may be discarded or changed so that it will conform pricewise to the rest of the line. The piece-goods buyer will be consulted to determine if lower priced fabrics might be available for possible substitution. Perhaps the designer can simplify or reduce the amount of trimming. If the changes are so drastic that the design will be ruined, it is often best to discard the sample. Even the most successful designer will always have a certain number of discards, samples which for one reason or another are never shown to the buyer.

Let us assume now, however, that our dress has passed the first test of style and price and is slated for production. The sample is immediately sketched and assigned a style number, by which it will be identified from now on. Next, the patternmaker begins his work. He drafts a complete pattern for production. When his pattern is completed, a duplicate sample is made, which is then checked against the original sample. The duplicate should be approved by the designer, and any changes in proportion must be corrected. When the pattern has been perfected, it is graded into the various sizes of its particular size range. The man who does this job is called a grader. A recent development in this area is computerized grading. Digital data, representing the proportional changes in size, is programmed

COST SHEET

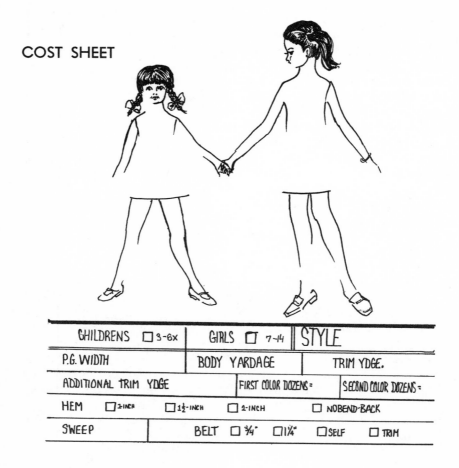

CHILDRENS ☐ 3-6x	GIRLS ☐ 7-14	STYLE	
P.G. WIDTH	BODY YARDAGE		TRIM YDGE.
ADDITIONAL TRIM YDGE	FIRST COLOR DOZENS =		SECOND COLOR DOZENS =
HEM ☐ ½-INCH ☐ 1½-INCH ☐ 2-INCH		☐ NOBEND-BACK	
SWEEP	BELT ☐ ¾" ☐ 1¼" ☐ SELF	☐ TRIM	

into a computer, and translated by the computer into directions for a cutting machine, which in turn cuts out the pattern automatically.

The graded pattern, now including all the pieces necessary for every size in its range, is arranged into a cutting layout called a marker. We also refer to the man who performs this task as a marker. He works on paper as wide as the fabric used for the garment, and manipulates the pattern pieces so that all fabric is utilized with as little waste as possible. Markers are from 50 to 100 feet long in order to accommodate all the pattern pieces necessary for a size range. Some large firms have photographic equipment which reduces all the pattern pieces to a fraction of their original size, so that the marker is planned in miniature. This gives a more efficient overview of the marker and allows for better utilization of fabric. Of course the completed marker must be enlarged again to full size before it can be used for cutting.

When the marker is completed, it is sent to the cutting department.

Here fabric is spread out on long tables, in layers of varying thickness, depending on the amount being cut. The marker is placed on the top layer, and the fabric is cut, according to the pattern outlines on the marker, with an electrically powered cutting machine. Small, intricately shaped pieces, such as collars, are often die cut to insure accuracy. The cut garments are now assorted to size, bundled, and ticketed in preparation for the sewing operations. Most progressive firms have an industrial engineer who supervises the breakdown of operations in the construction of a garment. Operators are usually paid for piece work. That is, they are paid a certain amount, agreed upon by the union shop steward and the production man, for each unit of work they complete. Operators are highly skilled and very fast in performing the particular task assigned to them. They need not necessarily know any of the other operations in putting a garment together.

Over the years, machines have been developed to combine many sewing

Rosenau Bros.

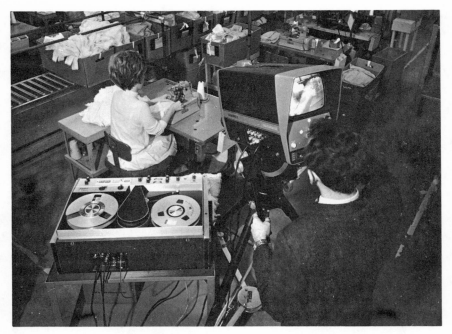

Methods study being taped on Instant Re-play T.V. at Her Majesty.

operations. There are machines to gather the cap of a sleeve and set it into the armhole in one operation. Machines fold bindings and finish raw edges at the same time. Multiple-needle machines can sew on many rows of trimming simultaneously. Collars can be set to the neckline and collar bindings attached automatically. Machines make buttonholes, and sew on all kinds of buttons. Wherever possible, automated procedures have been introduced into the manufacturing process, reducing the cost of production and making most efficient use of the increasingly limited numbers of skilled workers in the labor market.

The designer should be familiar with the machinery available for production, so that she can utilize its advantages in her designs. This does not mean that she should limit her thinking only to making use of the machinery in the plant, but occasionally minor adjustments can be made in a design to facilitate production. On the other hand, certain embroideries, appliqués, and other trimmings, too expensive to produce for some manufacturers when sent out to special embroidery firms, become feasible when the necessary machines are owned by the plant.

After the sewing process is completed, the garments are pressed and inspected for flaws before shipment. Most garments for children are now permanently pressed. This involves the use of fabrics constructed of natural fibers blended with polyesters and then treated with a chemical finish to impart permanent press qualities to the fabric after it has been heated under carefully controlled conditions. For children's dresses, blouses, and sportswear the heating step is usually delayed until the manufacturing process has been completed. After the finished garments have been pressed, they are placed on hangers and baked at the proper temperature so that the shape of the garment is set to last as long as the life of the fabric.

Children's garments are shipped in various ways. Outerwear, such as coats and jackets, gets no special handling before being placed in boxes for shipment. Dresses are often pinned over special cardboard frames for better hanger appeal when they are placed on racks in the stores. Blouses, underwear, sleepwear, and infants' clothing are usually folded and enclosed in cellophane or polyethylene bags before shipment. A complete picture of the garment, along with sizing and handling information for the consumer, is usually printed on the bag. This type of packaging keeps the product fresh and makes handling in the store much easier.

The manufacture of children's wear is a volume business. As the designer sees hundreds of dozens of her designs being shipped out of the firm, she experiences a thrill knowing that children all over the country, and often in other lands, will be wearing her garments. Often when she is travelling, or perhaps just walking along in the local park, she will see a child in one of her things, and somehow the knowledge that she has touched this child and perhaps brought her pleasure is one of the great rewards of designing for children.

NOTES

[1] 1897 *Sears, Roebuck Catalogue.* pp. 277, 278, 283.
[2] Louis Borgenicht as told to Harold Friedman. *The Happiest Man.* p. 230.
[3] *Ibid.* p. 336.

Chapter 4 / *Out of Thin Air?*

 CONSTANT flood of new ideas is essential. Without creative thinking, there would be no original garments, no new ways to clothe the human form, no fashion, and no fun in getting dressed. We assume that a designer is constantly bubbling with new ideas. Design-school training is limited to learning the skills necessary to give expression to the ideas. Courses are provided in sketching, patternmaking, draping, and sewing. It is quite obvious, however, that one can become an expert in all of these areas and still not be a designer.

You either have it or you don't! That is what many experts agree on when they discuss creativity, and it seems that they are correct when referring to the basic ability for original thinking. Most young children are creative. It is evident in their early art work, their original way of seeing the world and expressing their thoughts. Later, they become more inhibited, and original expression is often rejected in favor of the acceptable, proven response. Eventually drawings of people will look like other people's drawings of people, with eyes, nose, and mouth in all the right places, and with the acceptable lines for arms and legs. Dresses with rows of buttons, collars, and sleeves look like all the other acceptable dresses. Originality is being suppressed. The child produces work as good as everyone else's but not different. It is the rare person who can mature and acquire the skills of effective expression and communication without losing the talent for original creative thought. This is our potential designer. A designer is not afraid to express novel thoughts in new and different ways.

Assuming that our potential designer has all the creative prerequisites, let us consider the field of children's wear designing to see how this creative ability can be channeled into a commercially productive flow. Dress design is essentially a commercial art. Free expression is acceptable only as long as it is marketable. Without a market there is no job, and in the final analysis, there is not much satisfaction in making dresses that nobody is willing to buy.

To begin with, the designer must have a feeling for the times in which she lives. As our young people say, she must be "with it." Children don't live in a separate world. When the space age brings the streamlined design and functional materials of space suits to our TV screens, children's clothing will reflect some of this styling. On the other hand, when nostalgia invades the rest of the fashion field with ruffles and lace, children will be beruffled. Fashion changes constantly, but not in as capricious a way as is often supposed. There is steady evolution, reflecting the spirit of the world in which we live. The designer must acquire a sense of which way fashion is going, and which changes the public is ready to accept. Most people look for distinctive, rather than radically different, clothing. The new must somehow look right and not bizarre. It is interesting to note that a designer may have created a new, original dress, only to find that someone else has done the same thing simultaneously. Often copying is suspected, but in reality, both designers being exposed to the same events have responded in similar fashion and arrived at the same form of expression. As a rule, when a number of designers arrive at similar innovations in fashion as a response to current happenings, the public is ready for the change and will accept it enthusiastically.

Even the designer who is aware of the temper of current events and basically a creative person can have periods of low ebb, and find herself without any new ideas with which to work. In an industry where she is supposed to be evenly productive, and where a sample room full of workers depend on her creative output for their jobs, a creative slump can cause a major catastrophe. It is at these times that some deliberate analysis of the sources of inspiration can be helpful. Ideas do not come out of thin air. Gazing at the blank walls of a design room hardly produces anything but panic. So then, what are some of the sources of inspiration to which we can turn for children's wear?

Fabrics and Trimmings

Fabrics and trimmings inspire many designers. Various textures, colors, and prints may suggest ways in which they can be used effectively. Every season the textile houses prepare new lines from which the designer makes her selections. Almost every year brings some new chemical wonder to the fabric field, making clothing for children ever more serviceable and comfortable. Along with fabrics, new trimmings are constantly brought to the designer's attention. Representatives from the various trimming manufacturers present the latest in embroideries, laces, braids, and buttons. One never knows how the designer will react to a certain pattern, but this unique reaction is the basis for a new design.

Functionalism

Theoretically, the best inspiration for children's wear is the concept of Functionalism. This is the modern approach. The garments are designed to answer the needs created by the activities of the child. What are some of these thoroughly modern garments that children wear? There are snowsuits of lightweight, waterproof materials for play in winter; swimsuits that don't impede movement in water and dry quickly; sleepers of soft, warm, stretchable material with feet attached to keep the whole child snug and warm; stretchable colorful knit tights to keep little girls' legs warms and neat. The list is endless. Just consider the developmental needs and the activities of the child at school, at home, at sport and play, and certain features suggest themselves.

Current Fashion Trends

Current fashion trends, of course, are a major influence on children's wear. This impact of general fashion on the dress of children can take place in two ways. In one respect, the *general* feeling of a certain look filters into children's fashions. For example, the simplicity of the shift silhouette was perfect for children and won ready acceptance. There are many shifts for little girls, but although the general fashion is there, the individual interpretation may be quite different from anything done in the adult market. Again, when the nostalgia of the Edwardian look is popular for adults, little boys' and girls' clothing can be designed to have the same feeling for the period without being copied from the adult models.

Capitalizing on the desire of many schoolgirls to look like their older sisters, most manufacturers of 7-14 girls' wear like to give their lines a "Junior" look. That is, they want their designers to be thoroughly familiar with the Junior market and to capture this general feeling in their designs for the younger schoolgirl. This does not mean that miniaturized versions of Junior apparel are to be made for children. The proportions

and activities of children differ vastly from adults, and although a certain flair can be retained in the adaptation, the dress for the child must be designed with the child in mind.

In contrast to the general look of current fashion that filters down to children's wear, a designer can sometimes find inspiration in a *specific* style feature. An unusual pocket or a collar could suggest a child's dress which in no way resembles the adult garment in any other aspect. Sometimes a bow or a combination of colors can catch a designer's eye and then her own creativity takes over.

Of course there will always be some specific duplication. When trench coats are "in" for mother and dad, there will certainly be trench coats for son and daughter. When college girls wear ponchos over jeans, little sister will want a copy. Certain items lend themselves to all sizes and ages and look great on everyone. But beware, little girls just don't look so good in sexy satin dresses even if they are all the rage for Juniors.

To be thoroughly familiar with the current fashion picture, it is imperative that a designer get out of her studio or design room and shop the market. For anyone who works in New York or any other of the major cities this poses no problem. The large department and specialty stores display all the important new fashions. All types of apparel, from sportswear to evening gowns, should be studied anew every season. Only by repeated immersion in the current fashion scene can new trends be identified and become part of the thinking of the designer. Personal shopping tours should be supplemented by the current fashion publications. *Vogue* and *Harper's Bazaar*, as well as *Seventeen* and *Mademoiselle* for the Junior scene, should be read by every designer. *Women's Wear Daily*, the newspaper for the apparel industry, should be required reading, especially every Monday, when a section is devoted entirely to children's wear.

History

In the effort to create new and contemporary dress for the modern child, designers can also turn to the past for inspiration. Of course, we cannot really step back into history and bring back costumes as they were worn years ago. Life inevitably goes forward and the literal past is unretrievable along with the prim and proper outfits of yesterday's children. There are, however, trends in general fashion when certain historical periods extend their influence over the current scene. Sometimes this may be due to the success of a play or a motion picture. More often it is a combination of factors and events in our life which cause us to recall a certain historical period with nostalgic pleasure. Then designers will try to recreate in a new and contemporary way the fashions of that particular era. Perhaps it is the ruffled yoke of the turn of the century, the leg-o-

mutton sleeve of the Gibson girl, or the graceful lines of the French Empire which capture our fancy. It is a detail here or there, adapted from former times, which can give new charm to modern dress.

The designer can explore the past by studying the costume collections in the great museums. When no actual costumes are available, painting and sculpture of the past illustrate the various costumes worn throughout history. Richly illustrated books on the history of costume are available in the public libraries. Some of the larger libraries, notably the Main Branch of the New York Public Library, have excellent picture collections featuring fashion plates and photographs of fashions for men, women, and children from early antiquity to the more recent past. Television can also be an interesting source for the student of the twentieth-century fashion. Movie re-runs give us a lively view of the fashions of the 1930's, '40's, and '50's.

Folk Costume

Especially in designing outfits for children, ideas often come from folk costumes. Indian jackets with leather fringes, belts, and headbands have been popular. Oriental kimonos and mandarin gowns have inspired children's wear designers in the past. The Austrian peasants have lent us their aprons and puff-sleeved blouses as well as their dirndls for inspiration. Dutch and Scandinavian costumes, from hats to clogs, have given us ideas for all sorts of children's apparel. The field is vast. From Africans to Icelanders, from the Eskimos to the Incas, wherever individual cultures developed man has also created his unique costume. Children love the colors and the drama, and designers have a treasure of ideas to dip into whenever the mood is right.

Literature

A unique source of inspiration, especially for the designer of clothing for the very young child, is the field of children's literature. Fairy tales, from "Cinderella" to "Snow White," inspire dresses as well as designs for embroideries and appliqués. The nursery rhymes are an equally popular source of ideas. Often, the illustrations in children's books prove very fruitful. There have been countless *Alice in Wonderland* dresses and pinafores inspired by the Lewis Carroll classic. Perhaps the most striking example in this area is Kate Greenaway, who caused a real revolution in children's dress when her charming books for children appeared in England during the last two decades of the nineteenth century. In a period of constricting bustles and stays for adults, the children in her illustrations romped gayly across the pages of her books wearing the simple costume of the Empire period. As a result, the children of England and America, following her lead, were dressed in soft garments with tiny bodices and flowing sashes.

In designing a collection, most successful designers assess the mood of the moment and work around several inspirational themes. When a certain theme is repeated in various ways throughout a collection, the designer has made a positive statement about fashion. Isolated ideas, striking out timidly in new directions, usually get passed over by the buyers and in the end are meaningless. A valid, new idea, however, repeated in various ways always makes an impression. The merchant, who in turn must sell to the consumer, has a promotional idea with which to work. Inspirational themes lead to the design of groups of fashions that can be advertised and displayed together, usually leading to multiple sales on both the wholesale and the retail levels.

Chapter 5 / *The Designer as Buyer*

N a way, every designer is also a buyer. The piece-goods buyer and the trimming buyer may place the actual orders for stock, but the designer is responsible for the initial selection of the fabrics, trimmings, and notions used in the original sample garment. In the final analysis, it is the combination of these items that makes the design. These basic products must be carefully chosen so that the finished garment will be truly functional as well as fashionable.

Sales offices of firms producing fabrics and trimmings are located in New York City in the general vicinity of the garment center. The large fabric mills, such as Burlington, J. P. Stevens, and Lowenstein, are housed in their own new glass-and-steel skyscraper headquarters. On the other hand, many small converters and trimming houses operate from modest space in loft buildings. When shopping for fabrics, the designer should take periodic trips into the market. This is usually done before she begins to work on a new collection so that she can see the complete fabric lines for the new season. Textile firms schedule the designing of their lines so that they are ready with new textures, colors, and prints when the apparel designer needs them for her collection. At the fabric house, the designer is shown the entire fabric-merchandising story for the new season. New fashion colors have been developed and incorporated into coordinated groups of prints, woven patterns, and solids. These fabrics, designed to go together, lend themselves to combinations that can be used in a single garment, or in a group of garments to be displayed and sold together.

Despite the occasional trips to the fabric showrooms, most children's wear designers select practically all of the materials needed for the line right in their own offices and workrooms. Salesmen from the apparel manufacturer's established resources come to see the designer regularly so that they can supply samples of anything that may be needed. This includes embroideries, laces, buttons, belts, and other trimmings besides fabrics. If the time is not limited, a designer may spend almost every working day looking at lines. This, of course, is not appreciated by most employers, and it is wise to set aside only one or two mornings or afternoons a week for this purpose, Salesmen who call are notified at what time the designer will be available, and they make their appointments accordingly. When a designer, on the other hand, needs a particular item as she is working, she calls the appropriate house and her assigned salesman is usually only too happy to provide promptly whatever is required. It is extremely important for fabric and trimming salesmen to work efficiently with the designer. Only by supplying her with the samples that she wants can they hope to do business with the manufacturer when large orders are eventually placed for stock.

Naturally, not every sample that is ordered by the designer will be used. Sometimes a fabric swatch looks interesting, but the same material in a large piece turns out to be unattractive and just won't work in a garment. Now and then, laces and other trimming samples are ordered without a particular garment in mind in the hope that they will provide some future inspiration. The average sample cut may be anywhere from three to six yards of fabric depending on the type of garment, size range, and the manufacturer's general policy. Laces or braids are most often ordered in five-yard cuts. There is usually a charge to the manufacturer for samples of fabrics and trimmings. The small amounts involved and the extra handling required preclude any profit to the supplier. The manufacturer usually doesn't mind the cost, but when a designer orders indiscriminately, and large stockpiles of unused sample cuts and trimmings build up, most employers will not be very happy about their investment.

Fabrics

Fabrics, woven and knitted as well as the new urethane and vinyl films, are the basic raw materials of children's apparel. From the vast assortment of fabrics developed each season, the designer must select the right colors, textures, and weights for the garments that will be part of the new collection. The wearing and maintenance properties of the various fabrics are especially important in children's wear. Active children need clothing made from fabrics that can take rough wear and present no laundering problems. It is a rule with almost all children's wear manufacturers that fabrics used must be unconditionally washable. In addition, most fabrics have permanent press finishes so that, with modern home laundry equipment, maintenance of children's apparel requires a minimum of time and effort.

Our discussion in this chapter will be limited to the fabrics used mostly for children's wear. There is no attempt at general coverage of the vast field of textiles. Silks, linens, fine woolens, as well as some of the new synthetics, have been omitted here, because they are hardly ever used for children's apparel.

COTTON AND COTTON BLENDS

The natural fiber most widely used in children's apparel has traditionally been cotton. Cotton is probably the most versatile of all fibers. It can be woven or knitted into an almost endless variety of fabrics, with weights ranging from gossamer, silky organdy to heavy velveteen or corduroy coating. Cotton can be finished to have a soft hand, as in knits or flannelette, but cotton can also be crisp and starchy, as in poplin or pique. Cotton is used for every size range at every price level in every category of children's apparel.

Fabrics made of cotton are durable. Its fibers can be twisted very tightly into yarns that are strong and particularly noted for their abrasion resistance. This is the ability of a fabric to withstand the destructive effects of surface wear and rubbing. Cottons are temporarily even stronger when wet than when dry and are not damaged by hot water or strong laundry detergents. Since they also do not scorch easily and can be pressed with a hot iron, they can be laundered without special care. Although color fading and shrinkage were problems associated with cottons in the past, these disadvantages have been virtually eliminated by new dyeing methods that guarantee colorfastness and by shrinkage-control treatments that reduce residual shrinkage to less than one percent.

Cotton fabrics are comfortable. For summer clothing, cottons feel cool because they conduct heat away from the body. Since softly finished cotton is highly absorbent, it is particularly well suited for knitted underwear. Where fabrics made from other fibers may be clammy and irritating when wet, cotton absorbs perspiration and still keeps the wearer comfortable. This quality also makes cotton the ideal fiber for diapers. Furthermore, cotton fabrics can be used for warmth. The short fibers are brushed, raising the nap, thereby providing insulation for winter wear.

Cotton is plentiful in the United States, and therefore a relatively inexpensive fiber. This makes it particularly useful for children's wear. Youngsters are continually outgrowing their clothing, and most budget-minded parents look for inexpensive, practical outfits for their families. It must be added, however, that although the great bulk of cotton fabrics on the market is popularly priced, there are luxury types that are quite expensive. These are fine fabrics made from the long silky fibers of superior cotton plants. Although some luxury cottons are produced in the United States, the finest ones are imported. Some of the most beautiful cottons especially suited for children's wear are loomed in Switzerland. In addition to fiber quality, there are other factors contributing to the cost of cotton fabrics. One of these factors is the number of yarns per square inch of fabric. The rule here is, the higher the count the more expensive the fabric. The number of processes that the fabric goes through also adds to the selling price. Thus a fabric that has been improved by mercerizing and treated for shrinkage control and wrinkle resistance will cost more than an untreated fabric.

Many of the finishing processes that are commonly applied to cottons have been developed to counteract the disadvantages associated with cotton fabrics. Mercerization is a treatment of cotton fabric to increase its luster and enhance its affinity for dyes. Various shrinkage-control treatments, such as Sanforized and Paknit, among others, have been developed, and almost all cotton fabrics used for apparel now have dimensional stability, so that shrinkage is a problem of the past. The development of water-repellent finishes for cotton has made a revolutionary change in the selection of fabrics for outerwear. Lightweight cotton raincoats and jackets are now practical, and with a warm lining they are suitable for all seasons. The stain- and soil-resistant finishes are chemically similar to those developed for water repellency. They coat the surface of the fabric so that stains and soil cannot adhere and penetrate.

One of the traditional drawbacks of cotton fabric has been its tendency to wrinkle. For years, research has been devoted to the development of a finish that would improve the wrinkle resistance of cotton. Various processes, each an improvement over its predecessor, have been introduced since the end of World War II. When at last a truly effective permanent press process was developed, the abrasion resistance of cotton was substantially reduced. This resulted in fabrics that survived many washings without a wrinkle, but quickly wore through at stress points, such as the knees in pants and the elbows in shirts. Scientists eventually discovered that if the cotton fibers were blended with polyester fibers in the spinning process, the permanent press features remained and were even improved, and excellent abrasion resistance was retained in the fabric. Woven fabrics blended of 65 percent polyester and 35 percent cotton are now a staple in the children's wear industry. For knits, a blend of 50 percent polyester and 50 percent cotton is effective. When treated, these fabrics have excellent permanent press properties and combine the abrasion resistance of polyester with the comfort and versatility of cotton.

Other man-made fibers that have been successfully blended with cotton are nylon and high-wet-strength rayon. Nylon adds strength, abrasion resistance, and dimensional stability as well as a softer hand, better elasticity, and quick-drying qualities to cotton. Fabrics of nylon and cotton are especially effective for snowsuits and other outerwear. When the high-wet-strength rayon fibers are combined with cotton in a 50/50 blend, it is possible to achieve a fabric with the beauty, the hand, and the general quality of luxury cotton at a lower price. Both these blends take permanent press finishes effectively, and combine exceptionally good looks with the practical performance features required of all fabrics used for children's apparel.

Some of the cotton fabrics most often used for children's wear are listed below. All can be made in 100 percent cotton or blended with man-made fibers for increased strength and wrinkle resistance as well as more effective easy-care performance.

Batiste—A sheer fine fabric, woven of combed yarns and given a mercerized finish. It is used for lingerie, blouses, and infants' wear. A heavier type may be used for linings.

Organdy—A light, transparent fabric with a crisp finish. It may have a watermarked or moiré effect. The better qualities are made of pima or Egyptian cotton and are given a "permanent swiss finish." It comes in white or solid colors and can be printed. In children's wear, it is used most frequently for party dresses, alone or in combination with other fabrics.

Chambray—A smooth, durable cloth made of a dyed warp and unbleached or white filling. It is distinguished by an all-white selvage. It handles and wears well with excellent results in laundering. Chambray may be woven in stripes as well as solid colors. It is used for sportswear, dresses, or loungewear.

Gingham—Medium or fine yarns may be used to obtain the plaid, checked, or striped effects characteristic of gingham. The fabric is usually yarn dyed. Gingham is strong and serviceable. Depending on the finishes, it has a wide range in price. Designs range from conservative checks to traditional clan plaids and large bold patterns. Plaid gingham is a classic for back-to-school clothes and is used for dresses, skirts, jumpers, and other items of apparel.

Denim—This staple cotton cloth, both rugged and serviceable, is recognized by a steep twill on the face. Standard denim is made with blue warp yarn and gray or white filling. More recently, other colors have also been used. It is available in various weights and with permanent press and, occasionally, water-repellent finishes. Denim is a classic for sportswear and boys' wear. It is used for pants, jackets, skirts, and even coats.

Broadcloth—Cotton broadcloth is a soft, closely woven fabric with a slight filling rib. Good quality cloth has a smooth and satin-like finish. There is a wide variety of qualities in broadcloth, depending on construction, and care should be used in selection. It is used for dresses, blouses, shirts, slips, and boys' pajamas.

Percale—A staple cotton cloth of good fine texture. This compact, plain-weave fabric comes in white, solids, or prints. It withstands rugged wear and finds use in dresses, sportswear, and boys' wear.

Poplin—Cotton poplin has a more pronounced rib filling effect than broadcloth. The cloth is mercerized and usually additionally treated for a lustrous effect. It may be bleached or dyed with fadeproof colors; printed poplin is also popular. Heavy poplin is given a water-repellent finish for outdoor use. This versatile fabric is used in every area of children's wear from pajamas to raincoats.

Pique—A fabric characterized by heavy corded, ridged, or ribbed wales in the warp direction. It may also be woven into a waffle effect. Since it it is closely woven, it is relatively expensive for cotton material. Pique is used in children's wear whenever a firm fabric with some surface interest is desired. Traditionally, it has been used for contrasting collar and cuff sets.

Seersucker—A fabric with a pucker stripe effect that is achieved in the weaving process. Colored stripes are often used. This fabric launders well and needs no ironing. The crepe effect is permanent. It is used for lounge and sleepwear, boys' suits, and sportswear.

Plissé—Cotton fabric treated in a striped motif or in spot formation with a caustic soda solution, which shrinks part of the goods to provide the crinkled effect. This effect may or may not be removed after washing, depending on the quality of the fabric. Ironing, if done, should take place only after the fabric is thoroughly dry and with minimum pressure. Plissé is used mostly for summer sleepwear.

Flannel—A heavy soft cotton material that is given a napped finish on one or both sides. In a lighter weight with the nap on only one side, it is known as flannelette. It launders and handles well, but in the cheaper qualities, the nap may wear off after repeated washings. Flannel is made in solids, stripes, plaids, and prints. It is used for warm sleepwear, shirts, and linings.

Velveteen—A rich, low-pile cloth that comes in all colors, is mercerized, and has a durable texture. This strong fabric can be laundered, but will retain its beauty better when dry-cleaned. Velveteen provides warmth and tailors well. It is used for party dresses and jumpers as well as coats in all size ranges. Velveteen pile sheds at the cut edges; therefore all seams should be carefully finished, preferably with a binding, or the garment should be lined.

Corduroy—A hard-wearing pile fabric with a velvety ribbed surface effect. Corduroy may be woven with a plain-weave back or a twill back. The best corduroy has a closely woven twill back. There are several types of corduroy, depending upon the weight of the fabric and the width of the wales. Pinwale corduroy has very narrow wales and is relatively lightweight. Wide-wale, constitution, and cable are other descriptive terms for corduroy with wales of various widths. Corduroy is also available with no wales at all. It launders well. When corduroy is lined with thick pile or quilted fabrics, it is suitable for winter outerwear. When lined with flannel, its weight is ideal for jackets. Corduroy is also used for all other sportswear items as well as dresses and robes in all size ranges.

Cotton Suede—Also known as "duvetyne." The cloth is napped on one or both sides and is then sheared and brushed carefully in order to obtain the closely cropped nap that is characteristic of suede finishes. Cotton suede is an inexpensive substitute for suede leather. When the cloth is closely woven and the finish is good, it resembles suede so closely that it can be mistaken for the real thing. It is used in sportswear for jackets and coats as well as for jeans and skirts. It also is very effective as a trimming.

Terrycloth—This absorbent cotton fabric has uncut loops on both sides of the cloth. Its base may be woven or knitted. Woven terrycloth has a firmer hand and tailors well for bathrobes. Knitted terry will stretch; it is used for infants' wear, sweatshirts, and polo shirts. The cloth is of lighter weight and even more elastic when knitted of nylon or nylon blended with cotton.

Cotton Knits—Knit fabrics are becoming increasingly important in all types of apparel. The nature of the basic construction makes knit garments more comfortable, easy to maintain, and relatively inexpensive. Knitting produces a stretchable cloth, which makes garments that impose no restrictions on movement and usually provide some room for growth. Knit fabrics are porous and more absorbent than woven goods. Cotton knits vary in weight and texture from lightweight, smooth T-shirt material to the heavy napped fabric used for sweatshirts. Knits are made rapidly and the manufacturing process is flexible. Children's wear designers work closely with the mills in developing new patterns and effects. Special samples can be made up much more easily and quickly than with woven goods. There are two basic types of cotton knits:

Single-knitted fabric—Fabric knitted from one system of yarn. Several yarns may be combined, however, and passed into the machine as a single or individual yarn. Single-knitted cotton fabric is absorbent but usually lightweight and does not hold its shape. Given a finish for shrinkage control, it is suitable for knitted underwear or polo shirts. When single knits are used for dresses, they are usually bonded to an acetate backing in order to improve their hand and dimensional stability.

Double knits—A fabric knitted by interlocking loops on a double-needle machine so that it has double thickness. Both surfaces are somewhat riblike in appearance. Double knits are firmer and less stretchable than single knits. They drape well and are used for dresses and all items of sportswear.

WOOLENS AND WOOL BLENDS

Woolens have traditionally been used in children's apparel to provide warm clothing for winter wear. Woolen fabrics have body and resiliency. They are made with an endless variety of textures, from deep, soft fleecy naps for coatings to the lightweight, simple weaves used for trousers, skirts, jumpers, and dresses. Woolens have a remarkable affinity for dyes, so that colors range from deeply muted shades to the bright and light colors particularly good for children's wear. Woolen fabrics are comfortable in cool weather. The short fibers and the raised surface of most woolen cloths create air pockets that provide insulation to hold in body heat in cold climates. Woolen fibers are also porous and absorbent so that they never feel clammy when wet. Woolens are naturally wrinkle resistant; they press without any difficulty, and can be easily shaped in tailoring.

Although woolens have always been popular, there have been some drawbacks associated with their use in the past. Fabrics of 100 percent wool tend to shrink in the laundry, because the fibers felt when they are agitated. Various finishes have been applied to woolens in the past to make them washable, but not until blends were developed was the washability of wool fabrics substantially improved. The blending of polyester, acrylics, or nylon with the woolen fiber inhibits the felting tendency and imparts a dimensional stability which was not possible before. In addition, man-made fibers contribute abrasion resistance, strength, and durability as well as the ability to hold permanent pleats in woolen fabrics. These blends retain the hand, the warmth, and the absorbency of the woolen fiber but have brought along easier maintenance and good wearing qualties, characteristics essential for children's clothing. By and large, 100 percent woolen fabrics are used today only for children's coats, and even in this area, man-made fibers are being introduced and readily accepted by the public.

The designer should be aware of another problem associated with woolen fabrics. Many children are irritated by the somewhat scratchy texture of wool against the skin. For these children, woolen trousers or dresses must be lined or bonded. Skirts, jumpers, or coats cause no difficulty, because they do not touch the skin directly.

Some of the woolen fabrics most often used for children's wear are:

Plaid Wool—When the patterns are authentic clan plaids, these fabrics are also known as Tartans or Scotch plaids. Other novelty plaids might be muted, or pastel. These cloths are woven from woolen, worsted or blends in either plain or twill weave. For permanently pleated skirts, blends or combinations of wool with acrylic, nylon, or polyester give the best results. When combination yarns are used, and the pleats are formed on the lengthwise grain, the yarns containing the synthetic fiber should be used in the filling to ensure permanent press. If the synthetic yarns are used for the warp and run in the same direction as the pleats, they will have no effect on the pressed-crease retention of the woolen filling yarns, which have been pleated. Plaid woolens are traditionally used for back-to-school clothes, in skirts and jumpers for girls, and in trousers and sport jackets for boys.

Wool Flannel—A lightweight, soft woolen cloth with a dull finish. The napped surface conceals the weave. It is dyed in many colors, but gray and navy are perennial favorites for blazer jackets, pleated skirts, and trousers. The wool flannel used in children's wear is now mostly blended with nylon to improve the wearing quality and help maintain good press.

Wool Melton—A heavy coating with rigid construction that affords excellent wear. The heavy fulling or felting finishing treatments cover up all interlacings of the warp and filling, thereby making a genuinely "solid" cloth. Melton is used for peacoats and other outerwear for both boys and girls.

Chinchilla—The chief characteristic of this coating is its nub texture. In the finishing process, the fibers are actually curled into these chinchilla nubs. This closely woven fabric is warm and wears well. It is used for winter coats and heavy jackets for both boys and girls.

Wool Fleece—A heavy, compact, long-napped coating. Interlacings are well covered by the nap. The fabric is usually a good grade and provides excellent warmth. Children like the soft surface texture of fleece. The fabric is popular in all fashion colors but particularly in camel and navy.

Wool Knits—Both single and double knits are available in wool and various wool blends. Single knits are usually bonded to acetate for dimensional stability. These fabrics are rarely used for children's wear because they are relatively expensive. Bulky woolen knits, however, are still used for children's sweaters, but even in this area, acrylics are replacing woolens to a large extent.

RAYON AND ACETATE

Rayon and acetate are man-made cellulosic fibers. Both have as their basic ingredient natural plant materials, such as wood pulp and cotton linters. Rayon and acetate have, therefore, some of the same characteristics as natural fibers in that they are absorbent and pleasant to wear. They feel soft, are cool in warm weather and comfortably warm against the skin in winter. They are the least expensive fibers available, and are widely used alone and in combination with other fibers.

Rayon is the oldest man-made fiber. Although its inventors originally sought to create an artificial silk, rayon has its own useful and desirable characteristics and has nothing in common with silk. It blends beautifully with all other fibers. The new modified, high-wet-strength, and high-tenacity rayons are strong and wrinkle resistant, and they launder well. Rayon can be obtained in an unlimited range of colors. In children's wear, rayon's primary importance derives from the ease with which it is blended with cotton or wool. The versatility and generally desirable qualities of the natural fiber are retained, while the addition of rayon may reduce the price of the fabric considerably. By itself, rayon is also used in tricot for inexpensive girl's underwear and sleepwear.

Acetate is similar to rayon in that it starts out with the same cellulosic raw materials, but otherwise it has entirely different characteristics. Acetate has a particularly soft, luxurious hand. A brushed jersey of acetate feels soft, warm, and cuddly and is used for infants' receiving blankets, robes, and gowns. Acetate tricot is tremendously important as a backing in bonded fabrics. Single knits of all fibers acquire dimensional stability when bonded to acetate. Tweedy woolens that might feel scratchy against the skin become smoothly luxurious with acetate bonding. Openwork fabrics, which are too loosely structured to be either cut or sewn, become completely practical when bonded to acetate tricot. New processes are continually being developed that give additional dimensions to the uses of rayon and acetate. As their practical features of wearability are improved, and since their use in bonding and blending is constantly becoming more important, these fibers are assured a prominent place in the future of children's apparel.

THE SYNTHETICS

The synthetics are textiles constructed from fibers that are made by a chemical process. Basic chemicals are the raw materials for this wide variety of fabrics noted for their outstanding wearability and easy maintenance. Synthetics are rapidly becoming the most important fabrics for children's apparel. Alone or in combination with natural fibers, they are used in every type of garment available for children. There are many reasons for this phenomenal acceptance. Synthetic fibers soften at high temperatures, and fabrics may therefore be heat treated to set pleats, develop shape retention, or receive embossed designs. They are generally highly abrasion resistant and resilient. Since synthetic fibers are relatively non-absorbent, they all dry quickly. Synthetic fibers are non-allergenic and they are not affected by moths or mildew. The general advantages gained when synthetics are blended with natural fibers have already been mentioned. We shall now discuss the particular characteristics of some of the more widely used synthetic fibers in children's wear.

Nylon

First commercially produced in the United States in 1939, nylon is the oldest of the modern synthetics. The introduction of nylon brought with it an entirely new concept of what a fiber may be expected to do. Nylon filaments may be made fine or coarse, according to the needs of the fabric desired. Since nylon is exceptionally strong and yet lightweight, fabrics can be sheer and delicate but still practical. Nylon's abrasion resistance is three times that of wool. In addition, nylon is resilient: it springs back to its original dimensions after being stretched or compressed. Since nylon filaments are smooth and non-porous, they do not soil easily. Nylon is also non-absorbent; therefore it dries rapidly. Nylon fabrics made of filament yarn (the fine, smooth yarn made from continuous fibers with only a slight twist) have a silky, soft hand. On the other hand, nylon staple (filaments that have been cut into short lengths) can be spun into yarns that are used to create bulky, warm sweaters or lightweight, textured fabrics. Nylon has excellent dimensional stability, which is retained after repeated laundering. The ability to heat-set nylon makes permanent pleats and other surface effects, such as plisse, possible.

Nylon does have some drawbacks. The appearance of little balls on the surface of the fabric after repeated wearing is called pilling; it is a common fault of nylon and blends containing nylon. White nylon tends to turn grey unless it is rinsed repeatedly in the laundry process. Static electricity, which causes nylon blouses or sweaters to cling when the humidity is low, is a nuisance. This problem has been somewhat lessened by anti-static chemical finishes that can be applied to nylon. Lastly, the clammy feel of filament-nylon fabrics against the skin limits the uses of this fiber to some extent.

Nylon is used extensively in tricots for lingerie and sleepwear. Stretch nylon is used in children's hosiery and swimsuits, as well as in infants' stretchable garments. Tightly woven fabrics made from nylon fibers are used in water and wind-repellent snowsuits, ski apparel, windbreakers, raincoats, and sleeping bags. Outerwear is often designed with a shell of waterproof nylon fabric enclosing a polyester fiberfill interlining. This lightweight combination is warm and washable.

Acrylic

Acrylic is the generic name for all fibers made from a chemical compound called acrylonitrile. Acrylic fibers were first commercially produced in the United States in 1950. Some of the well known trademarks for acrylics include: Acrilan (Chemstrand), Creslan (American Cyanamid), Orlon (Du Pont), and Zefran (Dow). Acrylics are soft, warm, and bulky, somewhat wool-like in texture. They are lightweight but not as strong or as abrasion resistant as nylon. They have excellent pressed-crease retention and are moth resistant. They wash well with no special care and need little or no ironing. Acrylics can be used for the same type of apparel as woolens. Sweaters, socks, and accessories are knitted with acrylic yarn. Acrylics are used for double knits as well as for single knits bonded to acetate in all types of children's dresses and sportswear.

Modacrylic

Modacrylic fibers are similar to acrylics in that they also have as the basic ingredient acrylonitrile, but modacrylics have a smaller percentage of acrylonitrile, with other chemicals added to make this fiber. Modacrylics are used in apparel primarily for fur-like fabrics. Many variations have been developed. Some imitate natural furs, but others are unique in their construction. Children love the furry textures and lightweight warmth. The extremely low softening point of the fiber and its relative weakness require special care in handling. Garments should be dry-cleaned or washed in cool water by hand. Ironing, when needed, must be done at a low temperature. Trademarks for modacrylics are Dynel (Union Carbide) and Verel (Eastman).

Polyester

Polyester is the generic name for the fiber that has made permanent press a practical possibility. Although its commercial production dates back only to 1953, it has rapidly become what is possibly the most widely used synthetic fiber in children's wear. Some of the familiar trademarks for polyester are: Dacron (Du Pont), Fortrel (Fiber Industries), Kodel (Eastman), and Vicron (Beaunit). Fabrics made from polyester fibers may be smooth or nubby, in compact weaves, sturdy textured knits, or loose open knits. When tested for automatic wash-and-wear, polyester is rated excellent. Polyester fabrics retain their dimensional stability after repeated laundering and pleats remain permanently pressed. Polyester staples blend easily with other fibers, and they are commonly combined with cotton, wool, rayon, and acrylics to impart easy maintenance, strength, abrasion resistance, wrinkle-free appearance, and shape retention, while the natural fibers contribute dyeability, comfort, and absorbency.

Aside from the endless variety of blends available, lightweight woven 100 percent polyester fabrics are used for dresses, blouses, and boys' shirts. Most important, however, is 100 percent polyester double knit. This fabric with its miniature waffle surface texture is widely used in girls' dresses and sportswear. It has excellent body, drapes well, and comes in solid colors as well as stripes. Jacquard knits in several colors and interesting surface designs have also been developed. Polyester double knit washes easily and needs absolutely no ironing to retain its new look even after numerous launderings. Polyester is also widely used as a lightweight filling for insulated outer garments and in quilting for robes. This material, known by the trademarks Dacron Fiberfill or Fortrel Fiberfill, is warm, maintains its whiteness, does not absorb odors, and is non-allergenic.

Vinyl and Polyurethane Films

Although in the precise sense, vinyl and polyurethane films cannot be classified as textiles, they are becoming increasingly important for use in many items of children's clothing. Textiles, by definition, are constructed from fibers by weaving, knitting, crocheting, felting, or lace-making. None of these processes applies to film, a thin plastic sheeting that is flexible and drapeable. Film may be transparent and colorless, but it is also available in colors and prints. Since it is non-porous, vinyl film is absolutely waterproof. This makes it very useful as a material for diaper covers, babies' bibs or aprons, and also for really practical raincoats. Soft and flexible vinyls can be easily stitched on regular sewing machines, but since vinyls have a very low melting point, seams can also be fused together with applied heat, thus creating a truly watertight garment. Since vinyls are completely non-absorbent, they may be irritating to the skin. Therefore it is advisable that they be lined with fabric when used as raincoats or bibs.

Polyurethanes are now replacing vinyls in many areas. They don't become rigid and crack as easily as vinyls in low temperatures. Polyurethane also has porosity that vinyl lacks, making for more comfortable garments. Thin polyurethane film bonded to woven or knitted fabric provides certain features not necessarily associated with vinyl before. For example, transparent film bonded to the face of cotton makes this fabric waterproof. The shiny surface coating enhances the colors and patterns, and gives the fabric enough body to make it suitable for outerwear. Clear polyurethane film bonded to the back of fake fur keeps the wearer warm and dry. Even simple knits can be made waterproof when bonded to film and are suitable for diaper covers and other protective items.

Laminates

Laminated fabric is fabric that has been bonded to polyurethane foam. Any fabric can be bonded to foam and be transformed into a warm coating material. The foam acts as an insulator. New laminating techniques make these fabrics washable so that coats or jackets need no longer be dry-cleaned. In the past, these fabrics tended to be somewhat stiff, but the new methods are producing a more flexible, drapeable fabric. Laminated fabrics are relatively inexpensive. They are warm and lightweight.

"Sandwich Bond" refers to fabric in which a layer of polyurethane foam has been laminated between two fabrics. One is the face cloth and the other the lining. This eliminates the need for a separate lining and cuts down on labor costs. Laminated fabrics are being constantly improved. New bonding adhesives are becoming more permanent and flexible. Polyurethane foam now comes in a variety of weights so that the finished fabric can be soft and drapeable or have firm body, depending on the garment for which it will be used.

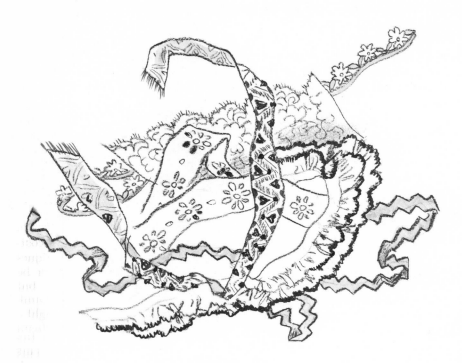

Trimmings

The great variety of design in children's clothing is to a large extent dependent on the use of trimmings. Once the basic shape of a garment has been developed, it is often repeated in various fabrics with different uses of trimmings. A basic dress might be cut in gingham, trimmed with eyelet; in double knit, trimmed with braid; in velveteen, trimmed with lace; and in organdy, trimmed with embroidery. Trimmings set the tone of a garment. A restrained, neatly tailored look can be achieved by using appropriate trimmings sparingly. Ruffles and lace give a feminine dressy air to a garment. Appliqués and embroideries can be whimsical or educational. Contrasting colors may be introduced with trimmings. Examples are: white eyelet ruffles framing the neckline of a dark dress or bright appliqués on serviceable overalls. Trimmings, when carefully used, can emphasize or underline certain design features of a garment. A pocket may be outlined with braid. Unusual seaming may be emphasized with lace or stitching. Trimmings may also be used to give a dainty finish to what might otherwise be troublesome raw edges, such as the lace edgings outlining ruffles, necklines, or sleeves where hems are clumsy or impossible, and facings would be inappropriate.

There are certain types of trimmings that are generally considered suitable for particular categories of children's apparel. On the whole, trimmings for boys' wear tend to be conservative. Excitement is created by contrasting colors and general cut. For small boys, appliqués and embroidery motifs depicting the objects in which boys are interested are commonly used. Airplanes, trains, whimsical animals, balls, and balloons, as well as sailboats and anchors, have always been popular. Stitching, creating a tailored effect, is used to trim shirts and pajamas.

For infants' wear, trimmings should be dainty and delicate. Narrow lace edging, delicate embroideries in pastel colors, smocking done by hand or by machine, very fine tucking and shirring, as well as narrow braids, are used to embellish babies' garments. Special care must be exercised in selecting trimmings for clothing worn by very young children so that they do not create a safety hazard. Decorations must be securely attached, and any loose ribbons or ties should be avoided.

For older girls, trimmings may be bolder. Bright contrasts give sparkle to garments. Certain trimmings can create a special look or effect. The use of rustic lace and colorful braid can make a peasant dress; fringe on a jacket gives an Indian look; and frog closings create an oriental air. Although trimmings on garments for older children may be colorful and more emphatic, they must nevertheless be in carefully chosen proportion to the finished garment and the child. Trimmings should never be overdone.

EMBROIDERY

From earliest times, man has used fancy stitching to embellish fabric. Embroidery was done with painstaking patience by hand, and considerable skill and artistry were developed to create beautiful designs, many of which are displayed in museums among the treasures of the world. Children's fashions in clothing, in many periods of history the exact miniatures of adult finery, have often made use of embroidery. Paintings, dating back many centuries, show children dressed in elaborately embroidered garments. Heirloom christening dresses are lavish with intricate handwork. Children's wear today still makes use of hand embroidery. Some luxury items are imported from countries where handwork is still available at a cost that is not too prohibitive. There are hand-embroidered infants' sweaters from Italy, christening dresses from France, and hand-smocked dresses from Puerto Rico or the Philippines. The demands of modern mass production, however, here and abroad, are responsible for the development of machine-made embroidery that compares favorably with the handmade product. Many types of machine embroidery lend themselves to children's apparel. We shall here attempt to discuss the embroideries that are generally suitable, pointing out in which areas of children's wear they are commonly used.

Hand Smocking

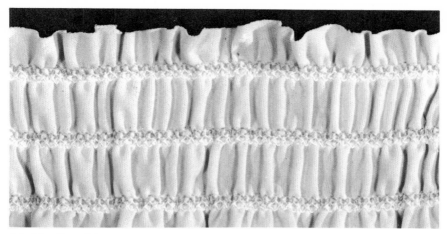

Machine Smocking

Smocking—Smocking is the use of embroidery stitches to hold gathered cloth in even folds. This type of embroidery has, for years, been typical of children's dresses, but recently it has also been used in adult fashions. Often the entire bodice of a child's dress is smocked. Designs are worked in over the gathered material. French knots, rosebuds, and other tiny motifs are used. Fabric can be gathered in even rows or in a diamond design. Smocking is still done by hand to a large extent. Some children's wear firms specialize in hand-smocked garments and manage to produce them at competitive prices. Machine smocking is available and much less expensive for volume production, but it hardly compares in beauty to the handmade product.

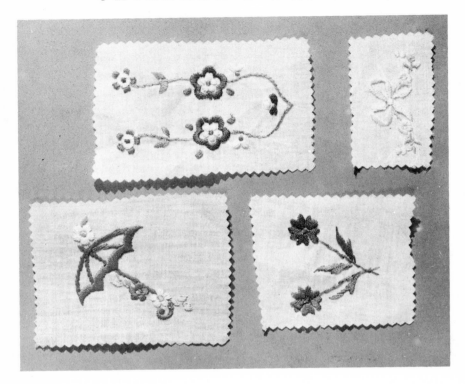

Handloom—One of the earliest types of machine-made embroidery, handloom is identical in appearance to hand embroidery. Heavy embroidery thread is used, and many colors can be incorporated in a design. Handloom embroidery is usually worked on the fabric section after it has been cut out. The front of the dress, the pockets, or the skirt, whichever piece the designer has chosen to embroider, is sent to the embroidery firm after cutting. Handloom embroidery motifs are limited in size to 3½ inches. That is the span of the handloom machine. There are also Grosloom machines that can execute designs up to 5 inches. The fabric is spanned on a frame and embroidered with a single stationary needle that goes back and forth through the fabric while the frame moves according to the design.

Schiffli—By the middle of the nineteenth century, the development of the schiffli embroidery machine in Switzerland caused a major revolution in the production of embroidery. The schiffli machine can stitch 10 to 15 yards of fabric at a time, using approximately 682 to 1030 needles simultaneously. The Swiss word *Schiffli* (translated "little boat") refers to the shape of the shuttle that is used in the machine. Its movements in coordination with the needles form a lockstitch that cannot ravel. The machine itself is a double decker, 10 to 15 yards long, and it operates somewhat like a sewing machine. The design is controlled by punched jacquard cards. This machine can embroider almost any pattern on either woven or knitted cloth as well as net. Recently, schiffli embroidery has also been applied to leather and lightweight plastic film. The schiffli machines can create an amazing variety of embroideries. Many fancy stitches are possible. Flat and relief work can be done. Eyelet embroidery as well as many types of laces can be produced Eyelet embroidery is particularly popular for children's wear. In this type of embroidery, holes of various shapes are first punched into the fabric and then finished along the edges with small, close stitches. These openings are worked in decorative designs and make a lacy, dainty trimming. Eyelet embroidery, as well as other types of schiffli embroidery, is sold in various forms.

All-over—This is a continuous pattern which covers the fabric from selvage to selvage with embroidery. The pattern may be connected or spaced. It may involve open work or plain embroidery. All-over patterns are sold on white batiste or may be worked on the manufacturer's fabric. For the dress designer, the stitching of samples may present a problem, because schiffli machines require 10½ yards of fabric to make a 10-yard sample. The machines cannot operate with less fabric. This means that extra-large sample cuts have to be ordered from the fabric house when schiffli embroidery is desired. Some schiffli producers have solved this problem by stitching various short lengths of fabric together to make up the 10-yard piece required by the machine. Others supply matching plain goods with their embroidery samples. In this way, the designer orders the exact yardage needed for the sample garment from the em-

broidery house. Later, fabric for stock is supplied by the usual resources. All-over embroidered fabric can be used for an entire garment or for only a small part, such as the front, or the collar and sleeves. Since embroidered fabric is more expensive than plain, combinations work out best when garments have to figure into a limited price range.

Edges—Embroidered edging is sold in various widths. These are narrow strips of embroidered fabric, usually batiste, which are finished with a continuous scallop on one side and left raw on the other. The raw edge may be gathered to create narrow, lacy ruffles, or be inserted flat into a seam.

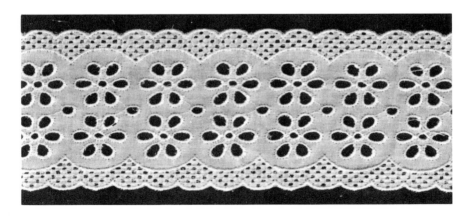

Galloon—An edge of varying widths which is decoratively finished with scallops on both sides of the embroidery.

Insertion—A trimming of varying widths that is sewn into the garment. Both sides of the embroidery are left unfinished for seam allowance. Sometimes there is a straight line on each side as a guide for sewing.

Band—A scalloped edge with a straight line on one side. The straight line serves as a sewing guide. When the fabric of the edging is cut close at the straight line, the edge is called a steel edge. Steel-edge finishes prevent ravelling and permit sewing the band on top of the fabric rather than inserting it into a seam.

Beading—A specially prepared edging, insertion, or galloon that has oblong eyelets through which ribbon may be run. Weaving ribbons by hand through beading is an expensive labor process. Therefore, beading has been developed where the eyelets are shaped so that the ribbon is merely stitched behind the beading, but the effect is just like laced ribbon.

Border—A design which consists of an embroidered motif along one side of the fabric. The fabric is not cut, but used full width. Scallops, which may or may not be cut, are sometimes used to finish the edge of the border design. Borders, whether they are embroidered or printed on the fabric, are always a challenge to the designer. In order to avoid costly fabric waste, the garment designed from the border fabric must utilize the decorated and plain parts of the fabric in the right proportion so that there is no excess of either after the dress has been cut.

Medallion—A single figure or design that has been stitched with reenforced edges to be cut out completely. Cutting is done by hand or machine. Medallions can be applied anywhere on a garment singly or in groups. Embroidered emblems and patches are also medallions. Application to the garment may involve high-frequency fusing, bonding, or conventional sewing methods. The new bonding methods achieve adhesion that remains permanent throughout repeated washing and dry-cleaning.

Jacquard Embroidery—This type of embroidery looks like schiffli embroidery. The process of execution, however, is entirely different. The jacquard embroidery machine consists of a group of lockstitch sewing machines joined together with a common shaft, and guided by a mechanical jacquard device. The operation of the machine is simple and does not require the use of a highly skilled operator. Therefore these machines are ideal for the manufacturer who wishes to do his own embroidery in his own plant. This eliminates the cost of shipping and saves valuable time in the production process. Jacquard machines can execute embroidery with the same results as the schiffli machine, with one exception. They cannot do eyelet embroidery. The work is very precise, since only small pieces of fabric are handled at a time.

Appliqué—The jacquard machine is ideally suited for appliqué embroidery. Appliqué embroidery is a type of ornamentation wherein a different piece of material, in an interesting shape, is sewn onto the base fabric with a close zigzag stitch. Jacquard or schiffli machines can combine appliqué with other embroidery in the same design. When the jacquard machine is used, the appliqué motif is die cut, backed, and then stitched to the base fabric. When executed on the schiffli machine, appliqués must be hand cut after the sewing process.

The designer must realize that the the use of embroidery will always add substantially to the cost of the garment. Shoddy embroidery is hardly worth any price, for it cheapens the garment on which it is used. When price is the primary consideration, it is best to keep embroidery to a minimum or eliminate it altogether. The quality of embroidery is determined by the number of stitches in the design. When stitches are small and close together, they form a solid, clean-looking pattern that will not unravel. This is particularly important in eyelet embroidery, for eyelets will fray when they are not finished with solid stitching. By eliminating stitches a design may be produced at a cheaper price. Any pattern can be made for less money, but only a limited number of stitches can reasonably be eliminated before the resulting embroidery looks shoddy and cheap. In addition, the type of thread and the number of colors used in the design also affect the cost of the embroidery.

LACE

By definition, lace is an openwork fabric produced by a network of threads twisted together, sometimes knotted, to form patterns. Traditionally, all lace was made entirely by hand from linen thread. By the nineteenth century cotton thread was more commonly used. Although lace-making machines had been invented by that time, handmade or "real" lace was still used in preference to the machine-made product. Today, however, handmade laces are considered collectors' items. The laces that are used in the various branches of the fashion industry are now all made by machines.

A machine patented in 1813 by John Leavers in England was able to produce laces that resembled the handmade product very closely. Today, the Leavers machine is still used, and in its modern form, it can create designs of infinite variety. For children's wear, the most commonly used

Leavers-type lace is Val, short for Valenciennes lace. This dainty, light, and airy lace, usually in the form of edgings, is used on all types of children's apparel. It is particularly suitable for infants' and toddlers' wear, and is almost indispensable in trimming children's lingerie. Val lace is now mostly made with nylon thread. When cotton thread is used, it is generally given a drip-dry, no-iron finish. Val is a flat bobbin lace with a diamond- or lozenge-shaped mesh ground. The lace is worked in one piece, and just one kind of thread is used for the outline of the design and every part of the fabric. The pattern is usually sprig-like or floral. In addition to the narrow edgings, Val is also available in the form of insertions, galloons, and beading.

Although traditional laces are always created with thread alone and without a ground fabric, many laces used for children's apparel are embroidered by the schiffli machine on a temporary ground fabric that is later removed by a chemical or heat process. Only the embroidered stitching remains. A large variety of laces can be imitated by the schiffli machine. Most popular for children's wear are the following:

Venice—A usually wide and quite heavy lace. The pattern is in the form of flowers and is united by bars. The design may be given a three-dimensional effect by raised embroidery stitching. Venice is available in galloons and edgings of various widths.

Tatting—Originally a knotted lace, it is now imitated by machine. Tatting is usually produced as a narrow edging, to be used as a dainty finish for ruffles, necklines, collars, and cuffs. It is particularly useful in the finishing of girls' lingerie.

Irish—A fine crocheted lace with rose or shamrock patterns that stand out from the background. Although Irish lace can be easily crocheted by hand, good-looking machine-made imitations are available for children's wear.

BRAID

Many types of trimming for children's apparel can be classified under the general category of braids. By definition, braids are narrow fabrics, sometimes rope-like, sometimes flat like ribbons, that are formed by weaving or plaiting together several strands of cotton, rayon, or other material. There are trimming houses that specialize in braids, and they supply the designer with the various trimmings listed below.

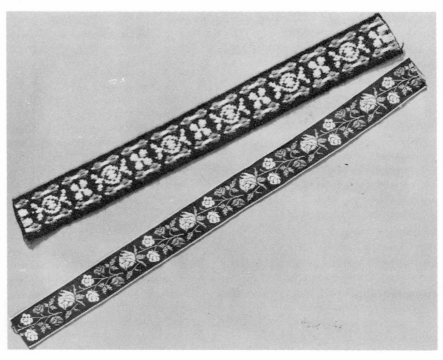

Peasant Braid—Peasant braid comes in various widths and is usually flat like a ribbon with textures that may be basically smooth or more rough and rustic. Peasant braids are usually embroidered with floral designs or other ethnic patterns in bright, clear colors. Sometimes the patterns are woven directly into the braid. When the peasant look is in fashion, which seems to be a recurring phenomenon every few years, peasant braids are used to trim every kind of apparel for both boys and girls of all ages.

Rickrack—This is a perennial favorite, an inexpensive trimming that is available in a wide range of sizes and can be dyed any color to match or contrast with all fabrics. Rickrack is woven into a zigzag shape. When rickrack is sewn on top of a fabric, it can be applied in several rows

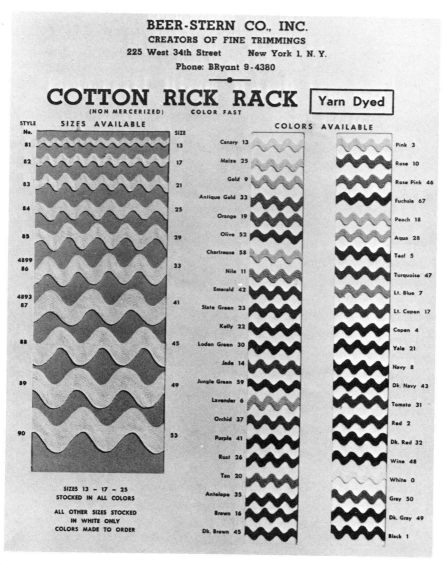

BEER-STERN CO., INC.
CREATORS OF FINE TRIMMINGS
225 West 34th Street   New York 1, N. Y.
Phone: BRyant 9-4380

COTTON RICK RACK | Yarn Dyed |
(NON MERCERIZED)   COLOR FAST

STYLE No.	SIZES AVAILABLE	SIZE	COLORS AVAILABLE		
81		13	Canary 13		Pink 3
82		17	Maize 25		Rose 10
83		21	Gold 9		Rose Pink 46
84		25	Antique Gold 33		Fuchsia 67
85		29	Orange 19		Peach 18
4899 86		33	Olive 52		Aqua 28
			Chartreuse 58		Teal 5
4893 87		41	Nile 11		Turquoise 47
			Emerald 42		Lt. Blue 7
88		45	Slate Green 23		Lt. Copen 17
			Kelly 22		Copen 4
			Loden Green 30		Yale 21
89		49	Jade 14		Navy 8
			Jungle Green 59		Dk. Navy 43
			Lavender 6		Tomato 31
			Orchid 37		Red 2
90		53	Purple 41		Dk. Red 32
			Rust 26		Wine 48
			Tan 20		White 0
			Antelope 35		Gray 50
			Brown 16		Dk. Gray 49
			Dk. Brown 45		Black 1

SIZES 13 — 17 — 25
STOCKED IN ALL COLORS

ALL OTHER SIZES STOCKED
IN WHITE ONLY
COLORS MADE TO ORDER

simultaneously with a multiple-needle machine, giving a bold but inexpensive trimming. It should be remembered that this type of application can only be done in straight lines, because multiple-needle machines cannot turn corners or stitch curves in one operation. However, rows of rickrack or other braids can be stitched around a skirt as a border or down the front of a blouse without any difficulty. Rickrack can also be inserted into seams or into the edges of collars and cuffs. When this is done, only the points of the rickrack will show to provide a dainty edging.

Soutache—This is a narrow, rounded, shiny braid, commonly woven of rayon or silk. Cotton braid of the same width is also available, and is more often used for children's wear. The cotton braid is flatter and has a herringbone effect in the weave. Soutache braid is so narrow, usually a quarter inch or less, that it can be curved and sewn around yokes, collars, and pockets. The traditional sailor collar is usually trimmed with two or three rows of soutache. These are applied with a multiple-needle machine and therefore must be stitched in straight lines without corners.

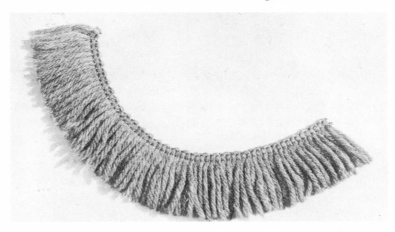

Fringe—Fringe is a decorative border of yarn or thread, hanging loosely from a ravelled edge of fabric or a separate band. Fringe may also consist of narrow strips of leather or plastic. The fringe that is sold as trimming is always attached to a band and sold by the yard. It is finished in various widths and thicknesses. The loops of yarn that form the fringe are sometimes left uncut for a novelty effect. All fringe should be securely attached to the band so that the loose yarns don't come off after washing and wearing. Fringe is effective in imparting an ethnic or nostalgic look to fashion.

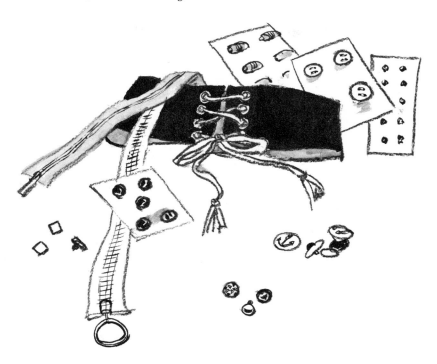

FASTENERS

The selection of fasteners required to finish garment openings can be routine or carefully considered by the designer. Often dress or jacket closings are handled as vital design features. There are numerous types of fastenings available for children's apparel. The designer has a choice of traditional or novelty buttons, a wide variety of zippers, and many kinds of gripper fasteners as well as grommets and eyelets for buckling and lacing.

Buttons that are passed through buttonholes or loops have been used traditionally for closing garments. There are two basic types of buttons. Sew-through buttons have two or four holes through which they are sewn to the garment. Shank buttons have a small projection or knob with holes on the underside of the button, through which the button is stitched. The shank may be in one piece with the button or may be a wire loop. Although shank buttons are considered more decorative than sew-throughs, since the buttons themselves are solid and the sewing thread is hidden from view, there are times when a shank button should not be used on children's apparel. By and large, the shank projection will become uncomfortable when these buttons are used for the back closing of a garment. On sleepwear also, a flat sew-through button is deemed to be more comfortable. Both sew-through and shank buttons are attached by special machines that can sew and space buttons automatically.

Buttons, whether shank or sew-through, come in many sizes. The diameter of a button is measured in lignes. A ligne is equal to 1/40 inch. Thus a sixteen-ligne button, a fairly common size for small garments, is equal to 2/5 inch in diameter; a 24-ligne button equals 3/5 inch: and a 30-ligne button equals ¾ inch.

Buttons can be both ornaments and fastenings. They are made from a large variety of materials, but for children's wear most buttons are made of plastic. Cellulose, casein and polystyrene, and the polyvinyl resins are used to manufacture buttons that can be molded into all sorts of decorative shapes. Molding machines can produce from 50,000 to 250,000 plastic buttons in a twenty-four-hour period. Plastic buttons can be clear and glass-like, or they can be dyed in a wide variety of brilliant colors. For the back opening on dresses or sportswear, a clear plastic sew-through button can be used on all types and colors of fabric. Plastic buttons are also made to simulate pearl, wood, metal, and other natural materials.

Silver- and gold-toned metal buttons are used on all sorts of children's wear. Metal sew-through buttons are available, but metal shank buttons are much more widely used. The face of the button may be smoothly polished with a shiny or brushed finish, or the metal can be embossed with all sorts of decorative designs. Anchor buttons for sailor suits are a typical example.

Real pearl buttons are still used on luxurious infants' garments, but for the most part, they have been replaced by the simulated pearl plastics. Nevertheless, real pearl buttons, especially ocean pearls, have a beautiful irridescence that can't quite be duplicated by the more common materials. Fresh-water pearls are somewhat less expensive than ocean pearls, but they do not have this highly irridescent quality. Pearl buttons can be white or dark grey. The dark grey pearl buttons are called "smoked" pearls. Sew-through pearl buttons or simulated pearls are used to fasten blouses and shirts. Tiny pearl shank buttons decorate little girls' party dresses, and larger pearl buttons are typical on toddler boys' suits.

For an occasional novelty effect, leather or wood buttons may be used. Since neither is washable, they are only suitable for outerwear that is normally dry-cleaned. Large, oblong buttons of leather or wood are called toggles. They are passed through loops rather than buttonholes, and they are typically used on duffle coats or on other rugged winter jackets. Recently, toggles made of plastic have also been introduced into the market.

There are a number of reasons why a designer might chose a zipper

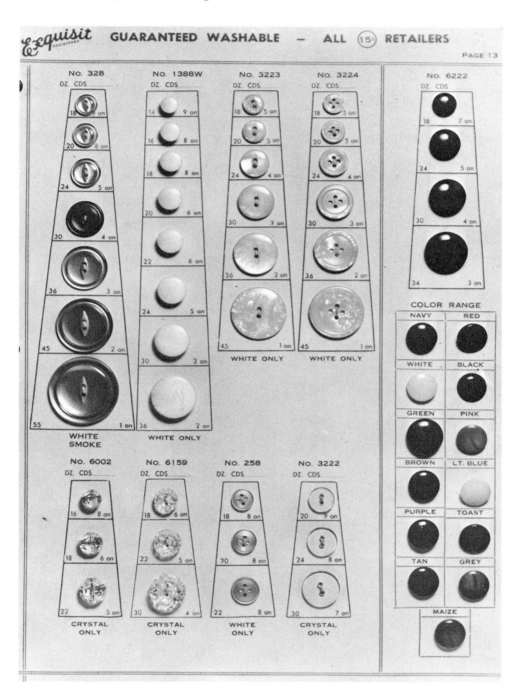

Exquisit GUARANTEED WASHABLE — ALL ⑮ RETAILERS

PAGE 13

No. 328	No. 1388W	No. 3223	No. 3224	No. 6222

WHITE SMOKE — WHITE ONLY — WHITE ONLY — WHITE ONLY

COLOR RANGE

NAVY	RED
WHITE	BLACK
GREEN	PINK
BROWN	LT. BLUE
PURPLE	TOAST
TAN	GREY

MAIZE

No. 6002	No. 6159	No. 258	No. 3222

CRYSTAL ONLY — CRYSTAL ONLY — WHITE ONLY — CRYSTAL ONLY

SCOVILL

GRIPPER® **Snap Fasteners**

------------------------ SPECIAL DESIGN CAPS ------------------------

#3391/16
Checkerboard

#3188/16
Plume

#3225/16
Flower

#3187/16
Pointed Petal

#3439/17
Block

#3449/17
Target

#3450/17
Parallel Lines

#3409/17
Checkerboard

#3441/19
Ship's Wheel

#3283/19
Crossed Pistols

#3321/19
Crossed Racquets

#3322/19
Cap, Bat & Ball

#3325/19
Dog

#3334/19
Fish

#3323/19
Bucking Bronco
(Raised)

#3320/19
West Cal. 45

#3366/19
Horse & Rider

#3256 19
Cowboy

#3231/19
Bucking Bronco
(Sunken)

#3324/19
Saddle

#3235/19
Nested Crescent

#3472/19
Circle

#3448/19
Geometric

#3240 19
Horseshoe & Star

#3284/19
Stallion

#3287/19
Horse Head

#3205/19
Stipple

#3237/19
Checkerboard

#3501/19
Bubble

#3447/19
Starburst

#3500/19
Stars

#3528/19
Saturn

#3196 19
Raised Rim

#3524/19
Lined

#3342 19
Rosette

#3239/19
Nickel-Gilt
or Enamel

#3442/19
Hammered

#3503 19
Sunburst

#3390/24
Nickel-Gilt
or Enamel

#3355/24
Lined

#3410 24
Chessman

#3420/28
Nickel-Gilt
or Enamel

#3384/28
Crown

#3523/28
Sew-Button

SCOVILL MANUFACTURING COMPANY
CLOSURE DIVISION
WATERBURY, CONNECTICUT

rather than buttons to close a child's garment. Zippers can be more easily managed by a young child just learning to dress alone. Once a zipper is properly closed, it will not pop open as buttons might do. Zippers provide a smooth, unobtrusive closing when used on the back of a dress. Zippers can close outerwear so that it is airtight and waterproof. Decorative zippers give apparel a modern streamlined air. Zippers are now designed with decorated tapes. Colorful patterns are printed on or woven into these tapes. The zipper itself may be in bright, contrasting colors. Separating zippers are used on jackets and coats. Regular zippers, which have one end securely fastened together, are used on neck openings, slacks, skirt plackets, and even on pockets.

Zippers were originally made of metal, but now nylon and other plastic materials are also used. Nylon zippers are lightweight and very fine, but after repeated laundering, they tend to come apart. The zipper people claim that by moving the slide the zipper can easily be repaired, but the average consumer seems to have difficulty with this, and for a sturdy long-lasting product, nothing has yet been able to outwear the traditional metal zipper. Especially on outerwear, the separating metal zipper is most often used.

Wide plastic zippers are very decorative and come in several colors. They often don't work as smoothly as metal zippers, and since they are as yet mostly imported, there are occasional problems of delivery. They do, however, provide a bright splash of color and are a very effective trimming.

Gripper-snap fasteners are sturdy modern snaps that are used on all types of garments for children. Originally, their use was confined mostly to sleepers, jeans, and the crotch openings in infants' pants, but recent fashion trends have made gripper snappers acceptable on all sorts of clothing from robes to raincoats and every type of sportswear. Front heads of the grippers are decorated with all kinds of fancy designs from embossed metal emblems to colorful enamel or jewel-like plastic inserts. Gripper heads are usually round, but interesting shapes are also available.

There are hand gadgets available for attaching grippers in the design room. The fastener people usually supply these tools to the designer. For factory use, efficient machines do the application. Gripper-snap fasteners are also sold spaced evenly on tapes, so that they can be easily sewn into garments without special machinery. Diaper pants, sleepers, and infants' wear crotch openings are often closed with these gripper tapes.

Metal eyelets or grommets for lacing or hooking fabric together can also be inserted into garments. The method of insertion is similar to that for the insertion of grippers.

The intelligent selection of fabrics and trimmings is vital to the success of the designer. In order to produce marketable garments continuously, the designer must make every effort to know about all the recent developments in the ever-changing field of textiles. As a result of the constant emergence of new products, fashions evolve and have become increasingly functional. The future will probably again bring more new and exciting fabrics—fabrics that will lend themselves to true mass production. With the constant decline of skilled personnel available, the stitching and assembling of garments by conventional methods will give way to new methods of production. These new methods will make cutting and sewing a luxury, as fabrics that can be molded and fused will eventually lead to the more economical production. Trimmings and fastenings must also keep pace with these new materials. The designer will have opportunity to create truly modern garments by taking advantage of the advances in the new textile technology. This is only the beginning. Fashion will continue to change rapidly and radically until the ultimate in good looks, comfort, ease of care, and economical production is achieved. Whether or not this stage will ever come to pass is anybody's guess, but until then, the designers must continue to work towards this goal.

PART II

Creative Patternmaking

Chapter 6 / *Basic Patternmaking*

THE following section is devoted to the basic patternmaking techniques used in children's wear design. Although designing with the flat pattern is universally accepted in the industry, it has become increasingly evident that certain shapes are more easily developed when draped directly in fabric on the dress form. Therefore many designers use both draping and patternmaking to translate their ideas into garments. Whereas most designers of adult fashions drape in muslin, in children's wear muslin is rarely used for this purpose. Most firms don't even have muslin available, but this is no particular disadvantage, since draping directly in the fabric of the finished garment gives the designer a clearer picture of the developing style as she drapes and cuts. Instructions for fabric draping are included at the end of this section.

Every designer should be familiar with basic patternmaking as it applies to children's wear. Once the foundation pattern has been draped, the styling of the basic bodice and skirt can be accomplished faster and more efficiently on the flat, rather than by redraping every variation. Basic sleeves and collars are easily drafted. Later, refinements of line can be achieved by trying the drafted pattern on the dress form and making corrections.

Since most firms employ a patternmaker to draft the perfect stock pattern, it is usually permissible for the designer to work with a fairly rough pattern, frequently making corrections as the sample is developed. When pattern shapes turn out to be unusual, such as a new collar or a unique pocket, most designers submit this pattern to the patternmaker along with the finished sample. This eliminates much trial and error for the patternmaker, and assures the designer of accurate reproduction of the design.

Although instructions for patterns in this book do not mention seam allowances, they must be added to all pieces before they are cut in fabric. The general rule for seam allowances is ½ inch for all basic seams. Necklines or enclosed seams, such as the inside seams in collars and cuffs, are ¼ inch. Some manufacturers prefer ⅜-inch seams, and others want ⅝ to ¾ of an inch on certain items. This depends on the price level of the garment and the special type of machinery used in production.

Tools for Patternmaking

Before beginning the specific instructions for patternmaking, a discussion of the required tools is in order.

SCISSORS AND SHEARS

Two pairs are needed. One pair should be reserved only for fabric-cutting and draping. For this dual purpose, medium-weight scissors with a 5-inch blade are usually satisfactory. Another pair of scissors should be used only for paper-cutting. Any scissors used for this purpose will become too dull for cutting fabric and draping. The paper shears may be somewhat heavier and larger. It is easier to develop the steady hand needed to achieve a smooth edge, essential for patterns, with generously proportioned shears. Good quality scissors and shears are worth the additional cost, and they must be kept sharp and in good working order.

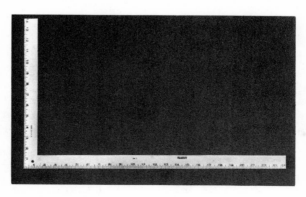

THE L SQUARE

This is an L-shaped ruler with arms at a perfect right angle. It is essential for marking grain lines on paper and for general patternmaking.

THE FRENCH CURVE

This clear plastic curved shape is engineered to facilitate the shaping of necklines, armholes, and other curved lines on patterns.

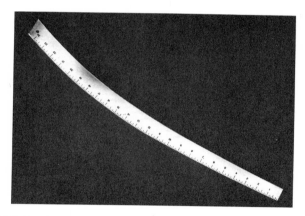

THE SKIRT CURVE

This curved ruler is particularly engineered to shape the side seams of skirts and shifts. It is also useful for shaping waistlines and other shallow curves in the pattern.

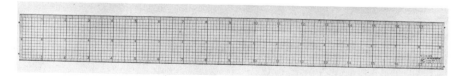

THE CLEAR PLASTIC RULER

These flexible rulers come in 1- and 2-inch widths, and are marked off in ¼-inch squares. They are very useful for adding seam allowances and are convenient for all sorts of measuring jobs.

THE TAPE MEASURE

This flexible tape is mainly used for measuring the figure.

PINS

Pins used for draping and general purposes should be lightweight and of good quality. Number 17 steel satin pins are recommended.

THE NEEDLE-POINT TRACING WHEEL

This is used to trace lines when developing a paper pattern.

THE DRESS FORM

The dress form is a facsimile of the human body used for the fitting and draping of garments. It is modelled according to the specific measurements of each size. There are dress forms consisting of only the torso on a stand, and there are full-length figures which reproduce the human

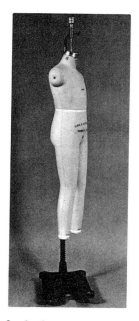
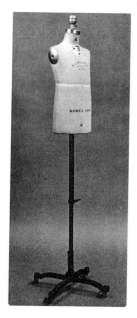

body from neck to ankle. Full-length leg forms are essential for designing sports wear and boys' wear. Some designers prefer a full-length form for all types of children's wear, since it gives a clearer picture of the proportion of the garment in relation to the size of the child. Full-length forms are considerably more expensive than dress forms. Therefore most manufacturers are likely to have only dress forms available in all sample sizes.

Dress forms are molded of papier-mâché, covered with a layer of wadding and jersey, and finished with an Irish linen canvas. The canvas cover is seamed in a conventional way, in order to serve as a guide for the placement of darts and seams in the garment. All forms have a seam at the center front and center back. There is a seam at the base of the neck and the shoulder. The canvas cover is joined at the side seam with a whipstitch, creating a ridge, which is easily located when draping. The conventional waistline is indicated with a tape. This is somewhat arbitrary in the smaller sizes, since young children don't have a natural waistline.

Dress forms in the larger sizes, beginning with the 7-14 size range, have a vertical seam separating the center front from the side front panel, and the center back from the side back. This seam is sometimes referred to as the "princess seam," since it is the characteristic fitting line of princess dresses, jackets, and coats, etc. The place where the arm joins the body is indicated on most dress forms with a metal plate, usually referred to as the armplate. Instead of an armplate, some forms, especially those used for outerwear, have a padded extension to indicate the top of the arm. Dress forms can be ordered with collapsible shoulders to facilitate the putting on and taking off of finished garments.

The Foundation Patterns

Every manufacturer has his own foundation patterns. These are basic patterns, fitted to the figure and perfected in the various sample sizes. These foundations, or slopers, as they are called in industry, are jealously guarded by most manufacturers, because they reveal his unique refinements in sizing and fit. Nevertheless it is important for the designer to be able to develop new foundation patterns when necessary. Slopers can be drafted from measurements, but are usually more quickly and accurately draped on the dress form. The usual group of slopers includes a basic waist, fitted with darts; a dartless shift; and a basic sleeve pattern. The basic sleeve pattern is drafted from measurements. Then it is cut in muslin and fitted to the waist for any necessary adjustments. Muslin is the fabric used to drape the foundation. Accuracy is essential, and muslin readily reveals any flaws in grain position and fit.

THE BASIC WAIST

Preparation of muslin:
1. Tear two pieces of muslin measuring:
   length—distance of center back from neckline to waistline
   + 4 inches.
   width—width across back at underarm + 3 inches.

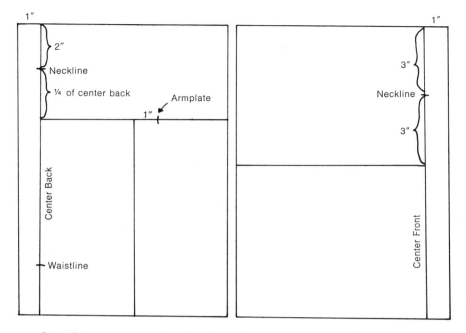

2. Straighten grain so that length and cross grain in muslin are perfectly perpendicular, and press carefully.

3. Draw a grainline 1 inch from edge of muslin for center front and center back.

4. On center back, measure down 2 inches from top of muslin to locate neckline.

5. From this point measure down center back to locate waistline.

6. Measure down from neckline one quarter of the center back measurement to locate the level of the shoulder blades.

7. Draw a cross-grain line at this level.

8. On this cross-grain line, mark off the distance between the center back and the armplate.

9. On the cross-grain line, measure 1 inch toward center back from armplate. From this point drop a grain line to lower edge of muslin.

10. On center front, measure down 3 inches from top of muslin to locate neckline.

11. From this point, measure down 3 inches for level of cross-grain line across chest.

Front:

1. Pin at center front and neckline intersection.

2. Pin at center front and waistline intersection.

3. Smooth muslin cross grain across upper chest area and pin at arm-hole.

4. Smooth down around armhole and pin at intersection of side seam and armhole.
5. Smooth lightly, with grain, down along side front section of bodice, and pin at the center point between side seam and dart, taking in a slight pinch for ease.
6. Take in excess muslin for waistline dart. Distance between finished dart and center front at waistline should range proportionately from

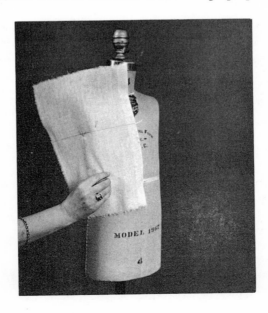

about 2¼ inches for a size 2, to 3 inches for a size 10. Actual dart pick-up may be very small on sizes 3-6x, and even smaller on 1-3. Infants' garments need no dart at all. Locate vanishing point of dart with a pin.

7. Slash and shape neckline (see photo), making sure that grain is not

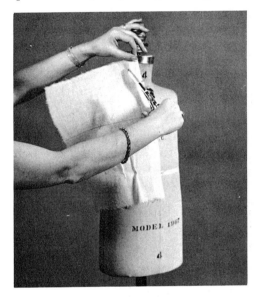

stretched in the neckline area. (Always smooth in the direction of the grain as muslin is slashed for neckline.)

8. Pin shoulder into place at neckline and armhole intersections.

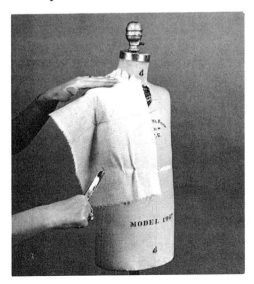

9. Mark, as shown in diagram.
   a. Dot neckline.
   b. Crossmark at neckline and shoulder.
   c. Crossmark at armhole ridge and shoulder.
   d. Dot to screw level along armhole ridge.

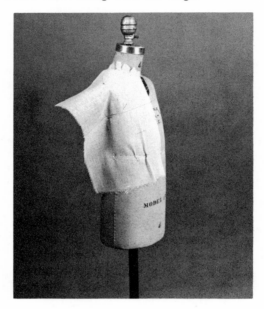

   e. Crossmark at underarm and side seam.
   f. Crossmark at waistline and side seam.
   g. Dot waistline to dart.
   h. Crossmark both sides of dart at waistline.
   i. Crossmark at center front and waistline
10. Remove from figure.
11. True:
    a. Extend center of dart on grain from waistline to level of vanishing point. Adjust position of vanishing point if necessary. Connect both sides of dart from waistline to vanishing point.
    b. Lower neckline ¼ inch at center front. True neckline with French curve.
    c. Establish shoulder line by connecting crossmarks at neckline and armhole ridge.
    d. Connect crossmarks at side seam from armhole to waistline.
    e. To enlarge the armhole for a set-in sleeve, measure down from armhole ridge at shoulder, over the center of the plate, to the side seam (see photo). Armhole depth should measure 4½ inches for size 10, 4⅜ inches for size 8, 4 inches for size 4, and 3¾ inches for size 2. The size of the armhole plate varies according to the

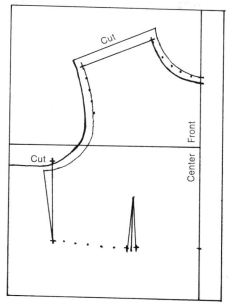

manufacturer and the age of the dress form. Therefore the distance between the bottom edge of the plate and the recommended arm-hole depth may vary from ¼ inch on some dress forms to 1½ inches on some older models. Lower armhole at side seam accordingly.

f. Extend side seam ½ inch at lowered armhole for ease in all size

ranges except 7-14. Sizes 7-14 need a ¾-inch extension for proper fit. From this point connect new side seam to waistline and original side seam intersection.

   g. True armhole with French curve, connecting shoulder, dotted ridge, and lowered armhole.

12. Pin dart.
13. Add ½-inch seam allowance on all seams except at neckline. Necklines need only a ¼-inch seam allowance.
14. Cut out front of waist at neckline, armhole, and shoulder.

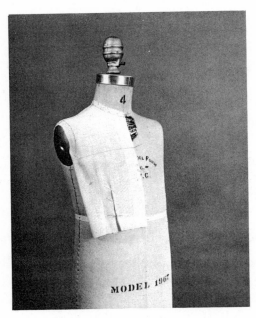

15. Replace on dress form as illustrated. Shoulder seam should be marked with a dark pencil line and pinned down smoothly so that back of waist can be draped over the front in the shoulder area. Instead of pinning side seam to dress form at side seam, pin 1 inch away from side seam toward front so that side-seam area on dress form is exposed for draping the back.

Back:
1. Prepare muslin for back as illustrated.
2. Pin to dress form at center back.
3. Smooth grain across shoulder-blade area leaving a slight amount of ease and pin at armhole plate.
4. Smooth grain downward at indicated grain line and pin at waistline with a pinch for ease.
5. Pin excess fullness at waistline for dart, placing back dart the same

distance from center back as front dart is from center front. Back dart pick-up will be greater than front dart.

6. Indicate the level of the vanishing point of the dart with a pin. Vanishing point of the dart should be at least ½ inch below the level of the arm plate.

7. Smoothing in the direction of the grain, slash and shape the back neckline. Pin at the intersection of shoulder and neckline.

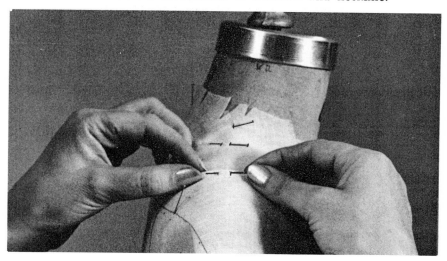

8. Smooth muslin up over front shoulder. Place two pinches (about ¹⁄₁₆ inch deep) along shoulder line. Back shoulder seam measures ¼ inch longer than front shoulder seam. Pin at armhole and shoulder intersection over front.

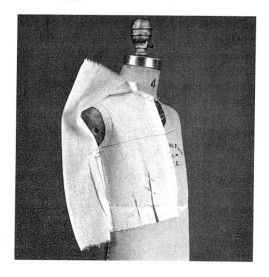

9. Locate back side seam by pinning to original (no ease) front side seam at underarm and waistline.

10. Mark:
    a. Dot neckline, shoulder, and waistline.
    b. Crossmark intersections at: neckline and shoulder, shoulder and armhole, waistline and center back, and arm plate at shoulder-blade level, both sides of dart at waistline.
11. True:
    a. Leave side seam pinned together and remove both front and back waist from dress form.
    b. Trace original and extended side seam from front to back waist.
    c. True back waistline dart same as front. Center of dart must be on grain.
    d. Connect dots for neckline and shoulder seam.
    e. Shape armhole by connecting crossmarks at shoulder, arm plate, and side seam with French curve. Armhole should follow the grain for about 1 inch below shoulder blade.
    f. Pin dart.
    g. Pin side seam together, and true the waistline of front and back with one continuous line. Grain should be straight from front dart to center front at waistline.
    h. Pin shoulder seam together easing back shoulder.
12. Replace on dress form; check fit; make any necesary adjustments.

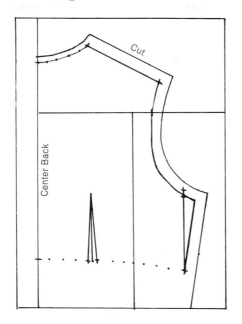

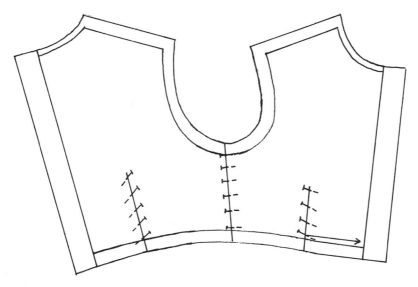

THE BASIC SHIFT WITHOUT DARTS

Eliminating darts provides for a smooth foundation, which simplifies patternmaking for almost any type of unfitted garment. This does, however, throw off the grain in the chest area, a factor that can be troublesome in the larger sizes of the 7-14 size range. The dartless shift is *not* suitable for Sub-teens unless cut in knits or other stretch fabrics.

Center Front

Center Back

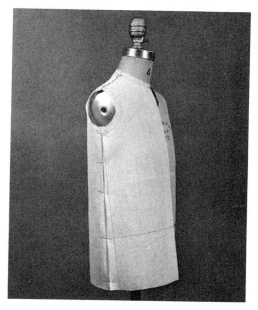

Preparation of muslin:
1. Tear two pieces of muslin measuring:
   length—center back from neckline to hem + 2 inches;
   width—across back at underarm + 4 inches.
2. Straighten grain so that length and cross grain in muslin are perfectly perpendicular, and press carefully.

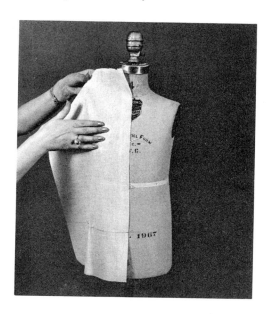

3. Draw a grain line 1 inch from edge of muslin for center front and center back.
4. Divide entire length of muslin into quarters.
5. Draw a cross-grain line at upper quarter of back.
6. Draw a cross-grain line at lower quarter of front.
7. On center back, measure down 2 inches from top of muslin to locate neckline.
8. On center front, measure down 4 inches from top of muslin to locate neckline.

Front:
1. Pin center front at neckline, chest, and indicated grain line.
2. Smooth across grain line and pin 3 to 4 inches from center front.
3. Pick up a ¼-inch pinch for ease along grain line.
4. Smooth up towards shoulder and place a row of pins across chest. Grain will be slightly higher at armhole than at center front.
5. Smooth up to neckline and shoulder; shape neckline.

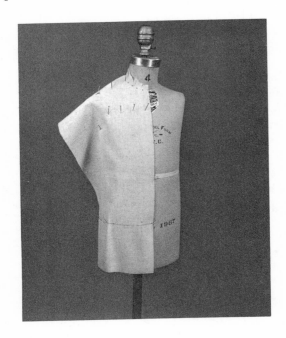

6. Pin shoulder into place at neckline and armhole intersections. There will be a slight amount of ease in the armhole.
7. Mark, as shown in diagram.
   a. Dot neckline.
   b. Crossmark at neckline and shoulder.
   c. Crossmark at armhole ridge and shoulder.

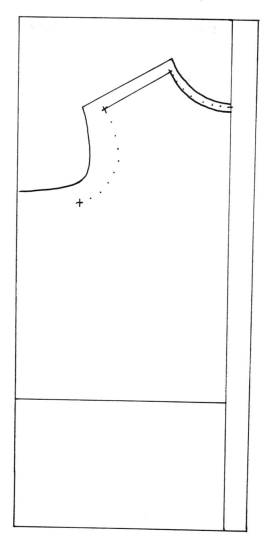

d. Dot armhole.

e. Crossmark at bottom of armplate and side seam.

8. Remove from dress form.
9. Lower neckline ¼ inch at center front; true neckline and shoulder.
10. Leave seam allowance and cut out neckline and shoulder.
11. Leaving about 1 inch, roughly cut out armhole.
12. Return to dress form and pin down center front and shoulder.
13. Pin center back at neckline, grainline, and torso.
14. Letting back fall straight down, smooth along grain line to armhole; pin along grain line.

15. Without disturbing the back grain, pin back and front together at side seam and armhole intersection.
16. Shape neckline and pin back shoulder over front. There will be ¼-inch ease in the back shoulder.
17. Mark: same as front of shift.
18. Remove both back and front from dress form.
19. *On back and front*, lower armhole for a set-in sleeve (See page 96 step 11-e) and extend ½ inch beyond side seam crossmark.
20. From enlarged armhole, drop grain line to hem.

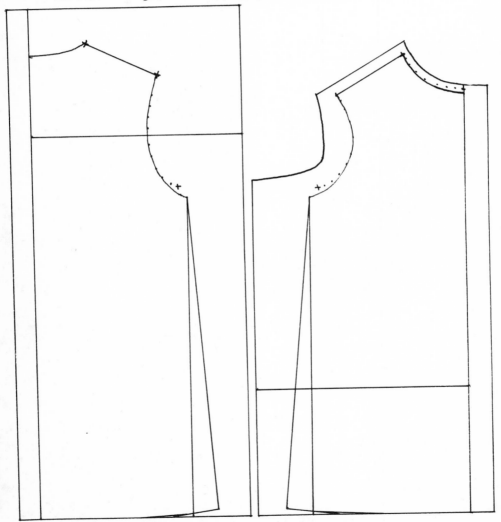

21. Add 1-inch flare at hem. (This is not really a flare but necessary ease for movement.)

22. Shape armhole front and back with French curve.
23. True back neckline and shoulder.
24. Pin side seam and shoulder together.
25. Replace on dress form; adjust hemline; check fit.

THE SLEEVE SLOPER

Table I—Sleeve Measurements for Sample Sizes in Children's Wear

						SUB-TEEN		
SIZES	2	4	6	8	10	8	10	12
Cap Height	3¼	3½	3⅞	4¼	4½	5¾	5⅞	6
Biceps Circumference	9¼	9¾	10⅛	11¼	11½	11	11½	12
Underarm	7⅝	9½	10	13¼	13¾	15¼	15⅝	16
Wrist Circumference	7	7½	8	8¼	8½	8	8¼	8½

1. Fold paper in half.
2. Square a line from fold representing the top of the sleeve.
3. Measure cap height down on fold to determine the level of the biceps.
4. Square a line from fold for biceps.
5. On this line, mark off half of biceps measurement.
6. On fold, mark underarm length down from biceps level.
7. Square up line for wrist.

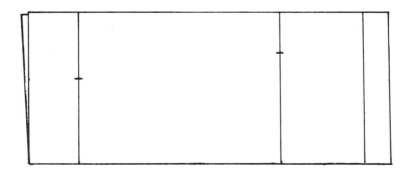

8. On this line, mark off half of wrist measurement.

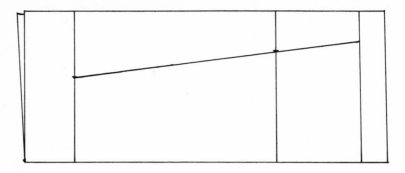

9. Connect wrist and biceps, extending line to top of sleeve.

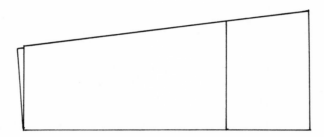

10. Cut out sleeve.

To Shape Cap:
  1. Fold sleeve cap in quarters.
  2. Mark in ½ inch at top of cap.

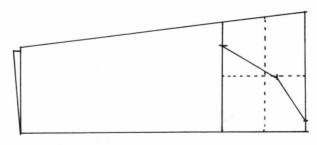

3. Mark ½ inch up, toward top of sleeve, from folded intersection.
4. Mark in from underarm line 1 inch at biceps level.
5. Connect guide points lightly.
6. For final shaping, place French curve so that upper cap rounds off above guide lines.

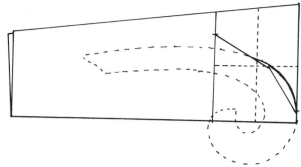

7. To shape lower cap, trace through front armhole section from basic waist as illustrated.

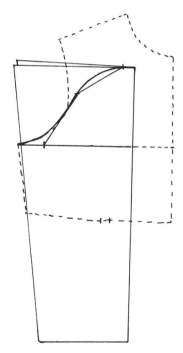

8. Add ⅛ inch along curve of back cap for ease.

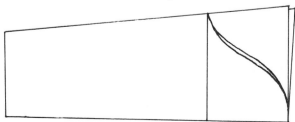

9. Trace front of cap to other side of pattern.
10. Cut out cap.

To Shape Elbow:

For most children's sleeves a straight sloper is sufficient. When, however, a more fitted sleeve is desirable, as in a full-length dress or jacket sleeve, the elbow must be shaped and the wrist tapered.

1. Locate elbow by measuring 1 inch above the halfway point between biceps and wrist.

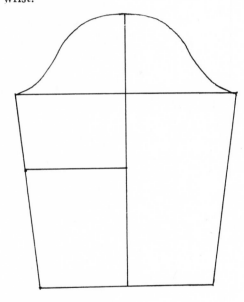

2. Slash at elbow to center of sleeve.
3. Spread slash to ¾-inch opening, shaping in wrist at the same time.
4. Extra fullness at elbow must be absorbed by shaping two small darts, gathers, or a tuck.

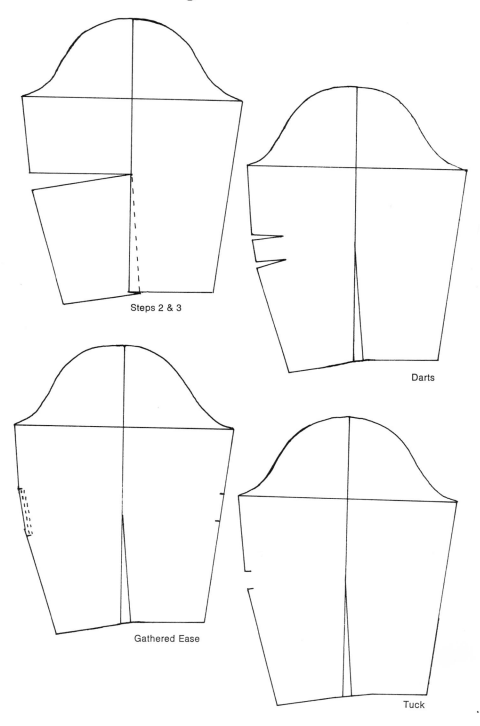

Steps 2 & 3

Darts

Gathered Ease

Tuck

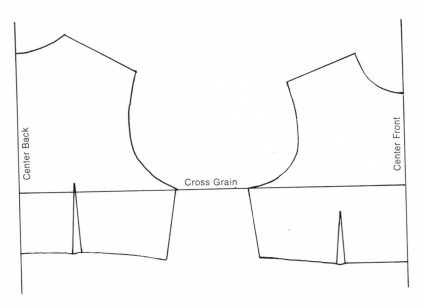

TRANSFERRING MUSLIN PATTERNS TO PAPER

When all the foundation patterns have been completed in muslin and checked for perfect fit on the dress form, they are transferred to thin, flexible cardboard or plastic sheeting so that they can be used repeatedly for developing other patterns.

To transfer muslin patterns:

1. Separate pattern pieces; open darts; true all corrections carefully; press flat without disturbing the grain.

2. Draw a cross-grain line across the back and front patterns at the intersection of the armhole and side seam.

3. On paper or plastic, draw two parallel lines, representing center back and center front, far enough apart so that front and back slopers can fit in between; draw a perpendicular line between center back and center front at the level of the underarm.

4. Place muslins on paper with center back, center front, and cross grain aligned; smooth the rest of the muslin pattern into place, and secure with pins or weights; trace carefully on seam lines with the spiked tracing wheel.

5. If seam allowances are desired, add them before cutting out the basic pattern. In the industry, most patternmakers work with seam allowances on their slopers. Many designers, however, find it easier to develop new patterns without taking seam allowances into consideration. It is perfectly acceptable to work either way. In this book, all patterns are developed from slopers without seam allowances.

Sleeve Variations

Since sleeves lend themselves to a variety of treatments, they are frequently the focal point of a child's garment. Sleeves can be narrow and small, or full and wide. Often they are made of contrasting fabric or adorned with trimming.

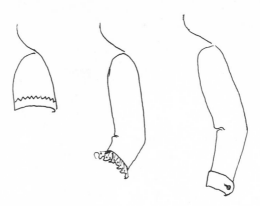

I. *STRAIGHT SLEEVES*, based on the basic sloper, can be cut at various lengths ranging from short to three-quarter and wrist-length sleeves.

To cut variations of the straight sleeve:

    1. Estimate length on traced sloper.

    2. Add hem or cuff and cut.

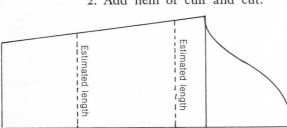
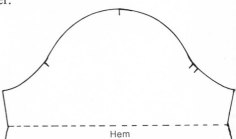

II. For a *VERY SHORT STRAIGHT SLEEVE*, eliminate some of of the fullness at the biceps of the sleeve sloper.

To cut the very short straight sleeve:

    1. Mark length of sleeve at center fold of sloper. Sleeve length should be at least ½ inch at underarm.

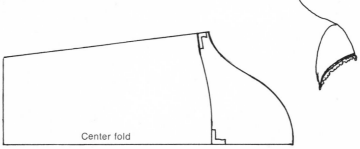

    2. To draw lower edge of sleeve, square off 1 inch from center-fold mark and 1 inch from underarm mark on sleeve sloper. Connect with a shallow curved line.

    3. Cut out sleeve.

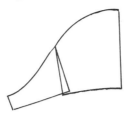

4. Slash sleeve halfway between center fold and underarm.
5. Overlap ¼ inch at lower edge. Since lower edge will curve, it needs a facing, or sleeve should be lined.

III. The *SHIRTWAIST SLEEVE* is very effective for children's wear. Basically a straight sleeve, it has enough fullness to permit easy movement. At the wrist, the extra fullness is gathered or pleated into a cuff. The sleeve cap is flattened, and almost all the extra ease is eliminated at the top of the sleeve.

To cut a shirtwaist sleeve:

1. Fold paper in half.
2. Square biceps line from fold.

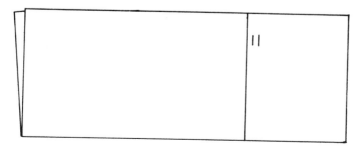

3. Place a short guideline ¼ inch above biceps and another line ¼ inch above this first guideline. The sleeve cap will be flattened ½ inch for this sleeve. This is an arbitrary measurement and may be varied slightly according to effect desired.

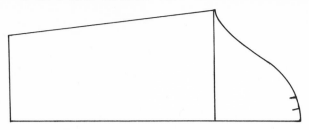

4. Mark off two ½-inch spaces from center of sleeve cap on the seam allowance of folded sloper.

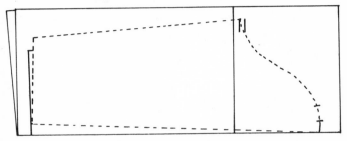

5. Place sloper on folded paper and trace cap to first ½-inch mark; trace wrist.
6. Using first mark as pivot point, swing biceps of sloper to first ¼-inch guideline of paper.

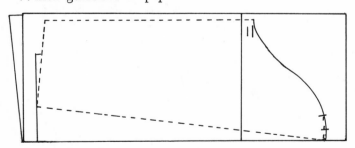

7. Trace cap to second ½-inch mark and pivot, using second mark as pivot point, so that biceps of sloper is in line with the second ¼-inch guideline on paper.
8. Trace rest of sleeve cap; measure cap. Compare to armhole; sleeve cap should be ½ inch longer than armhole.
   (If cap is too large, adjust necessary amount at underarm.)

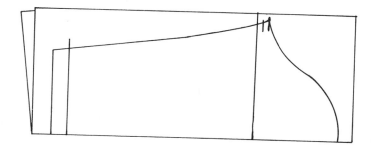

9. Connect underarm from biceps to wrist level, allowing for desired width of sleeve at wrist. When wrist is narrower than biceps, underarm seam should be curved as illustrated.
10. Shorten sleeve ¾ inch less than the finished width of the cuff. (Example: for a 2-inch cuff, the sleeve should be shortened 1¼ inches.)

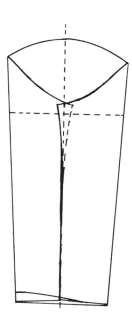

11. Cut out sleeve.
12. Fold sleeve in quarters as illustrated. When underarm seam is curved, seam will overlap at biceps.
13. Mark up ½ inch on front fold from wrist. Square 1-inch line across; mark 1 inch from fold on back wrist. Complete wrist by connecting markings and blending into a shallow S curve.
14. Cut out finished wrist.

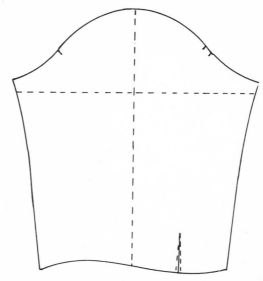

15. Open sleeve, mark up 2½ inches at back sleeve fold for slashed opening.

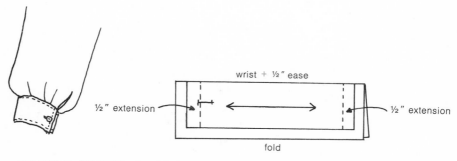

SIMPLE CUFFS should be planned with ½-inch ease at the wrist and grain running crosswise.

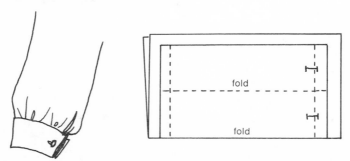

FRENCH CUFFS fold up and are cut double the width of the simple cuff.

IV. The *BISHOP SLEEVE* is similar to the shirtwaist sleeve, but the cap is not flattened, and there is more fullness in the lower part of the sleeve.

To cut a bishop sleeve:

1. Divide cap of folded sleeve sloper into three equal sections; divide wrist also into three equal sections.
2. Fold paper in half.

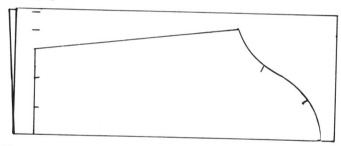

3. Place sloper on folded paper as illustrated.
4. At wrist level, on paper, mark desired width of lower sleeve.
5. Place another mark halfway between sloper and desired width at wrist.

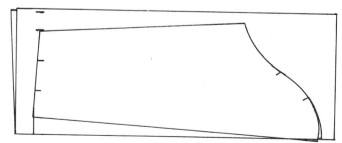

6. Beginning at center fold, trace first third of sleeve cap; trace first third of wrist.
7. Using first mark on sleeve cap as pivot point, swing out lower sleeve so that the underarm and wrist intersection touches the halfway mark on paper.

8. Trace middle section of cap and wrist.
9. Pivot from second mark on cap so that underarm and wrist intersection touches desired width of sleeve.

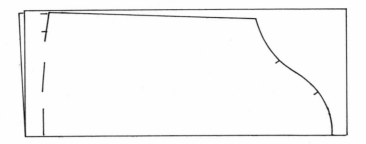

10. Trace last third of cap, entire underarm, and last third of wrist.
11. Connect wrist sections.
12. Follow directions for shirtwaist sleeve to finish lower edge * and cuff.

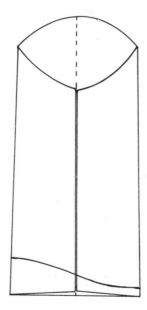

V. The *BABY DOLL SLEEVE* is a short version of the bishop sleeve. It is used on dresses as well as blouses and gives the effect of a soft puff with a smooth shoulder line.

* For more puffy fullness, allow 1-1½ inches additional length at back of sleeve.

To cut a baby doll sleeve:

1. Mark off desired length of sleeve on sloper.
2. Follow directions for bishop sleeve. Since this sleeve usually ends above the elbow, there is no need for special shaping of lower edge.

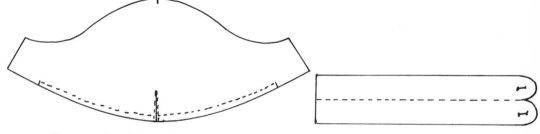

Pattern for baby doll sleeve and cuff. The same pattern, without gathers and cuff, is used for the *FLARED* or *BELL SLEEVE*.

VI. The *PUFFED SLEEVE*

For years, the sleeve most closely identified with children's wear has been the puffed sleeve. There are two basic types of puffed sleeve: the *PEASANT PUFF*, which may be constructed in any length and width, and the *SHORT BABY PUFF*, which needs no elastic or tight cuff to support it.

A. The *PEASANT PUFF SLEEVE*

To cut a peasant puff sleeve:

1. Estimate length and width of desired sleeve. Sheer, soft fabrics need more width.

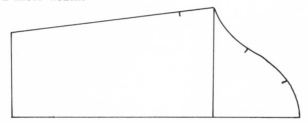

2. Mark off desired length at underarm of sleeve sloper. Sleeve may be short, three-quarter, or full length.

3. Divide cap of sleeve sloper into three equal sections.

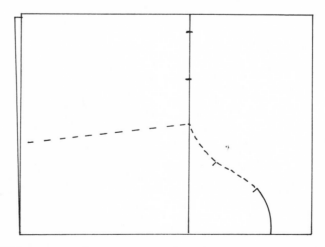

4. Fold paper and square up a line for biceps.

5. At biceps, mark off half of the estimated width of the sleeve.

6. Place sleeve sloper on paper and mark off half the distance between sloper and estimated width on biceps line.

7. Trace the first third of cap.

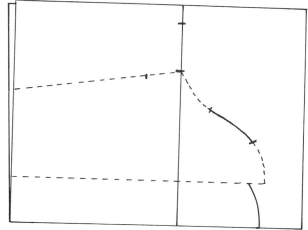

8. Shift sleeve sloper along biceps to first mark and trace the second third of cap.

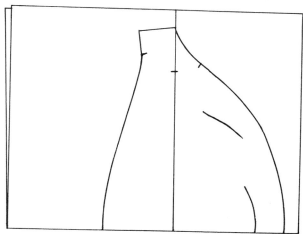

9. Shift sleeve sloper along biceps to the last mark, and trace the rest of cap and underarm, and square a 1-inch line from underarm for lower edge of sleeve.

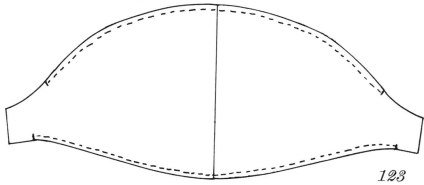

10. Taking into consideration the measurement estimated as the overall desired length of the puffed sleeve, add height at the cap and lower the bottom edge as illustrated. This will cause the sleeve to puff up at the cap and puff out at the lower edge when cap and lower edge are gathered to fit armhole and cuff. Lower edge may also be elasticized to fit the arm.

B. The *SHORT BABY PUFF*

This sleeve is typically associated with baby clothes and toddler wear. It is very short and perky without causing any pressure against the upper arm. It is usually finished with a French piping or a narrow cuff.

To cut a short baby puff sleeve:

1. Estimate length and width of puff sleeve same as for peasant sleeve. (Length approximately 6 inches for a size 4; 7 inches for a size 10.) Underarm should be no longer than 1 inch finished. (Width approximately 18 inches for a size 4; 20 inches for a size 10.)

2. Divide cap of sleeve sloper into three equal sections.

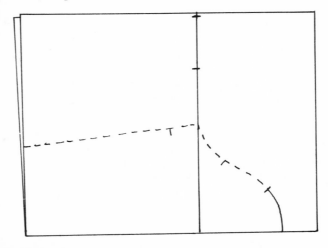

3. Fold paper and square up line for biceps.
4. At biceps, mark off half the estimated width of sleeve plus 1 inch.

5. Place sleeve sloper on paper, matching biceps line, and trace first third of cap.
6. On biceps line mark off half the distance between end of sloper and indicated mark for the width of sleeve.
7. Shift sleeve sloper to halfway mark along biceps, and trace second third of cap.
8. Shift sleeve sloper along biceps to full width of the sleeve. Using the last third mark on the sloper as a pivot point, drop the sloper 1 inch below the biceps line at the intersection of cap and underarm.

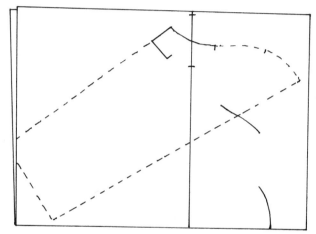

9. Trace in last third of sleeve cap and 1 inch of underarm seam.
10. Square 1 inch in from underarm seam for lower edge of sleeve.

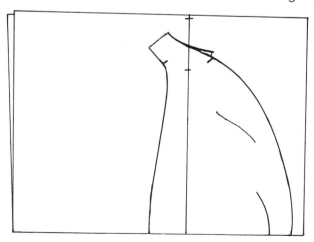

11. Using estimated desired length as a guide, shape cap above guidelines, and lower edge of sleeve as illustrated.

Collars

Almost all children's dresses, blouses, jackets, and coats are designed with some sort of collar. There are several reasons for this. To begin with, the collar draws attention to the face. In a way, it provides a frame setting off the child's features to best advantage. Women may transform a simple neckline with jewelry, and by the time they have reached their teens, they use make-up to highlight their features or brighten a dull complexion, but for children, this is considered in bad taste. For children, collars must be designed to provide the flattery of jewelry and cosmetics. Children's apparel of subdued or dark colors would be quite dreary if it were not for that touch of brightness near the face, often supplied by the contrasting collar. The crisp white collar of linen or pique looks right on many dresses. There are other instances, however, when a collar should be cut from the same fabric as the rest of the dress so as not to detract from other focal points of design. Collars are often trimmed with lace, embroidery, contrasting piping, or braid. Collars may be big like a Bertha or minute like a mandarin. They may stand high at the neck or lie flat on the shoulders. The variety is endless, limited only by the imagination of the designer.

Collars fall into two basic categories—the straight collars and the round collars.

I. *STRAIGHT COLLARS*

All straight collars are drafted from measurements. Measure the neckline of the garment (not the dress form or the child) from center back to shoulder, and from shoulder to center front.

A. *STRAIGHT SHIRT COLLAR—CONVERTIBLE*

1. Decide on desired width of collar. (Collar will be narrower in back since almost half the width will form the height of the roll.)
2. Fold paper in half as illustrated.
3. From fold, square a line across paper for the neckline of the collar.

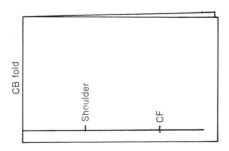

4. On this line, mark off the distance from center back to shoulder and from shoulder to center front.
5. On center back fold, measure up from neckline the desired width of the collar.

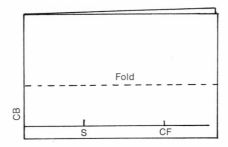

6. Square a line for the outer edge of the collar. This will be a fold line.
7. Refold paper as illustrated.

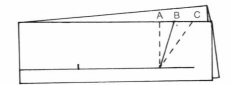

A   B   C

8. Draw in front edge of the collar. A squared line will give short points to the collar. The greater the angle of the front edge, the longer the points.

B. *BIAS ROLL COLLAR*

This collar is similar to the shirt collar, except that it is cut on the bias grain.

The back of the collar is usually split, shaped like the front, and allowed to lie flat.

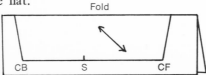

When cut in one piece, grain will not match in front.

To match stripes and plaids, collar must be cut in pairs as illustrated.

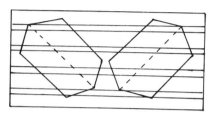

To make this collar conform still more to the neckline and lie a little flatter, the neck edge is curved slightly.

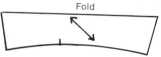

C. THE MANDARIN AND THE BAND COLLAR

A standing mandarin or band collar is shaped to fit the contour of the neck.

To cut a mandarin collar:

1. Fold paper as illustrated.
2. Square line across from fold ½ inch above lower edge.

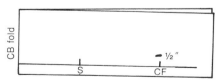

3. Center back is at fold. On line, mark off shoulder and center front of neckline.
4. Place mark ½ inch above center front.
5. Blend neckline as illustrated.

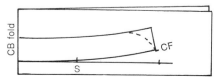

6. Draw parallel line for upper edge of collar.

7. Place on dress form and shape front edge as desired.

To cut a band collar:

1. Fold paper as illustrated. The fold is center front.

2. Square line across from fold ½ inch above lower edge.

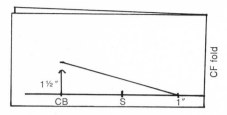

3. Mark off shoulder and center back.

4. Place mark 1½ inches above center back.

5. On line, place a mark 1 inch from center front.

6. Connect 1-inch mark with raised center back. Blend into shallow curve as illustrated.

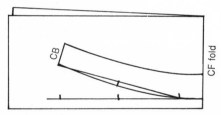

7. Square off center back from neckline.

8. Mark off finished width of band and draw upper edge of collar parallel to neckline as illustrated.

D. *THE TWO-PIECE SHIRT COLLAR*

This collar is the authentic shirt collar, and is used when a tailored effect is desired. Consisting of a band and an upper collar, it is fitted to the contour of the base of the neck. It is suitable for older girls.

To cut a two-piece shirt collar:

1. Band—Follow directions for mandarin collar, allowing for overlap extension at center front. The band may be shaped so that the back of the band is a little wider than the front.

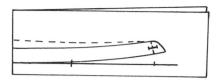

2. Collar—a. Trace upper curve of band to center front.

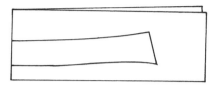

b. Shape the collar as desired. Collar should be at least ¼ inch wider at center back than the band.

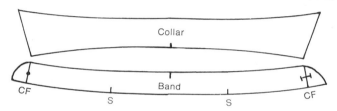

II. ROUND COLLARS

Round collars follow the neckline of the bodice pattern. Front and back bodice are placed so that the shoulder seam meets at the neckline intersection, and overlaps at least a ½ inch at the armhole intersection.

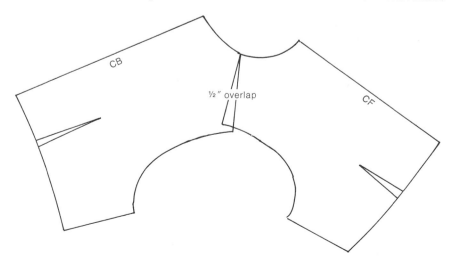

As the overlap at the shoulder tip increases, the neckline becomes straighter. The neckline is traced and becomes the neckline of the collar. A ½-inch overlap at the shoulder tip provides a neckline curve, which

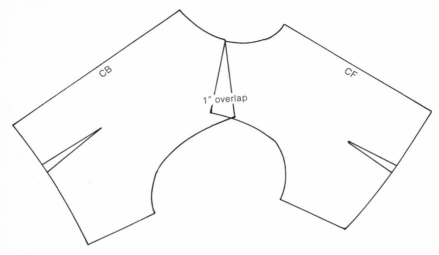

results in a fairly flat collar. A 1-inch overlap will result in a slight roll. The greater the overlap at the shoulder, the straighter the neckline, and the higher the roll of the collar.

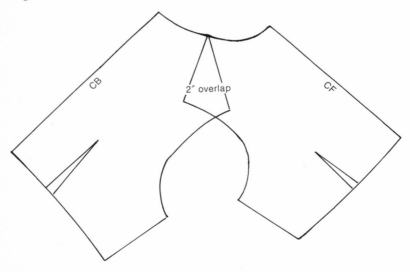

A. THE PETER PAN COLLAR

By far, the most popular collar for all children's wear is the Peter Pan collar. It curves gently around the neckline and can be finished with round or straight lines at the center front. At the center back, the collar may be split like the front to accommodate a back opening, or it may be cut in one piece.

To cut a Peter Pan collar:

1. For a flat collar, place front and back sloper with at least ½-inch overlap at shoulder and armhole intersection. When a more rolled collar is desired, overlap from 1 inch to 1½ inches.

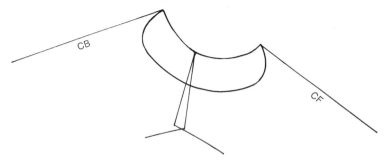

2. Trace neckline, center front, and center back, and indicate width of shoulder.

3. Shape Peter Pan collar as desired.

By changing the shape of the Peter Pan collar, we can design many variations.

B. BERTHA OR CAPE COLLAR

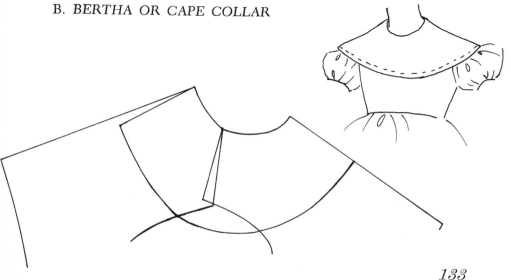

C. PURITAN COLLAR

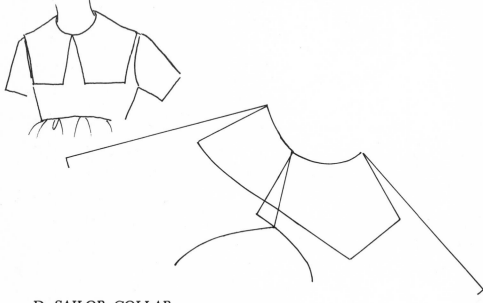

D. SAILOR COLLAR

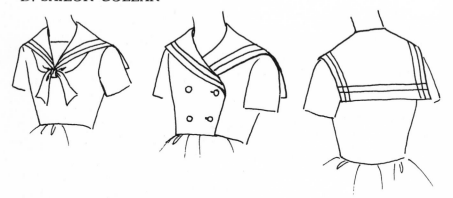

This classic shape is used for both boy's and girl's wear, with single- or double-breasted closings.

To cut a sailor collar:

1. Place front and back together with shoulders overlapping ½ inch at armhole.
2. Measure down length of collar at center back.
3. At this point, square line across back to armhole.
4. Square line up along armhole toward shoulder.
5. Connect with center front lowered neckline. Outer edge of collar may have to curve in front if neckline is not low enough.

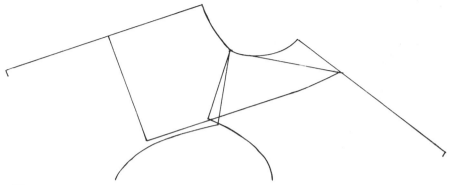

To cut a double-breasted sailor collar:
   1. Outline neckline and closing on front sloper.

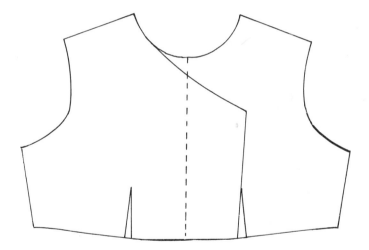

   2. Cut out front waist pattern, and place front and back together as for basic sailor collar.

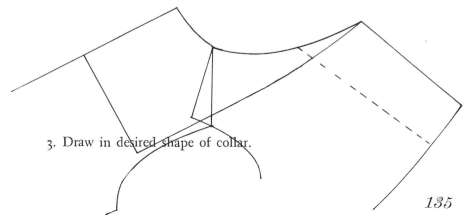

   3. Draw in desired shape of collar.

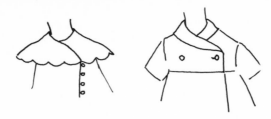

This method is used to design other collars with double-breasted closings. For higher roll, overlap at shoulder seam should increase proportionately.

The Princess

The fitted princess is a classic in children's wear. It is used in all types of apparel and for all size ranges. There are •princess dresses and coats ranging from Infants' to Sub-teen sizes. Princess lines fit tennis dresses and bathing suits as well as jackets and robes. The typical princess silhouette is fitted throughout the waist and has a flared skirt. The skirt width can vary from a modified A-line to a full circular flare. The position of the grain is most crucial in developing a princess pattern. The grain must be perfectly straight in every major pattern piece, with cross grain straight at the waistline, across the chest, and at hip level.

To cut the princess pattern:

1. Pin front and back of traced basic waist sloper on dress form and draw style lines as illustrated. (Princess-seam style lines should pass over, or be no more than ½ inch away from the apex of the waistline dart.) The style lines of the back waist should harmonize with the front. Back and front princess seams terminating at the shoulder seam should meet. If seams extend into the armhole, they should be at the same level.

2. Remove slopers from dress form and indicate three crossmarks,

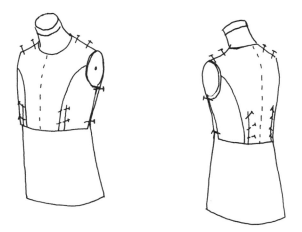

notches for matching seams, along the front princess line, and two crossmarks along the back princess line.

3. Separate center front and back from side sections. Cut away dart, shifting dart to conform to princess line where necessary.

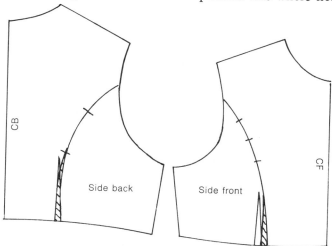

CB

Side back

Side front

CF

4. Working on a large piece of paper, draw line for center front.
5. Square line for waistline cross grain, from center front across the entire width of the paper.
6. Place center front panel on paper as illustrated, and trace.
7. From princess-seam and waistline intersection, extend grain line to hem level.
8. Add desired flare at hem level, and connect with princess seam at waistline. If point develops at waistline, smooth into a curve.
9. Place side front panel so that waistline rests against indicated grain line on paper, and trace. Allow enough space for skirt flare.
10. Draw parallel grain lines from waistline to hem level at princess seam and side seam.
11. Add flare to each side. Flare at princess seam must be equal to the flare at the princess seam at the center front panel so that the seam will be balanced. Side-seam flare need not equal princess-flare, but both sides of a single seam must be identical to assure straight position of seams on the finished garment.
12. Place side back and center back along waistline, following the same procedure as for front panels.
13. Add hem and seam allowance.
14. Cut out pattern. Be sure that all notches for matching seams are clearly marked.

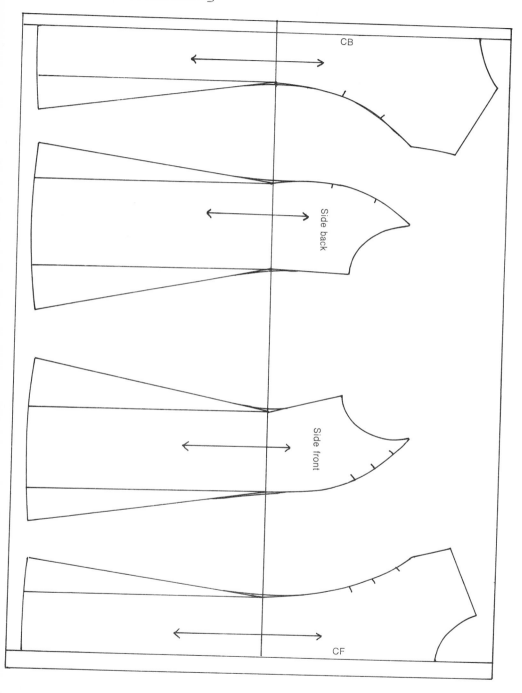

Variations of the Shift

Of all silhouettes for children's dresses, the shift most naturally follows the shape of the child's body. The comfortable, easy-fitting shift dress allows freedom of movement for active children. Its simple lines don't interfere with embroideries and other trimmings, and it is used for all sorts of dresses, from beach wear to party clothes. Fabrics used for shift dresses should have some body. The usual crisp cottons or firm wool-type fabrics are fine. Sheers or laces, suitable for party dresses, should be backed in order to maintain the shape of the shift.

The shape of the basic shift can be varied as follows. If not too much additional fullness is desired, changes can be achieved by shaping the side seam.

For a shaped A-line shift:

Indent side seam at waistline, and add up to 2 inches of flare at the hem level.

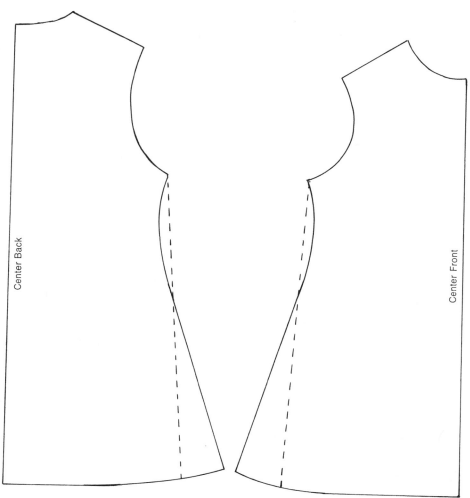

For a tent shape:

1. Mark off lower third of armhole on shift sloper (front and back).

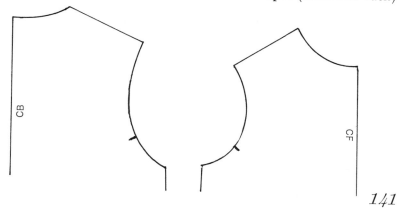

2. Place sloper on paper, and mark ¼ inch above armhole and side-seam intersection.

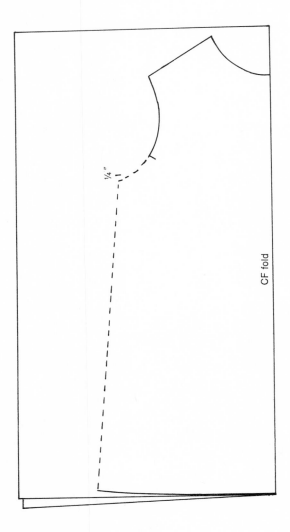

3. Trace center front, hem, neckline, shoulder, and upper two thirds of armhole.
4. Using mark on armhole as pivot point, shift armhole and side-seam intersection to ¼-inch mark on paper.
5. Trace lower third of armhole and side seam.
6. Up to 2 inches of additional fullness may be added at side seam if desired.

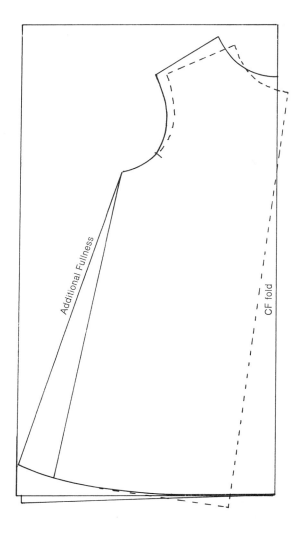

Yokes and Other Design Features

Once the basic silhouette for a garment has been established, most design in children's wear consists of adding style lines. These lines may be horizontal, vertical, or curved, adding interest and focal point to the design. Seams for yokes and other design features must be placed in just the right proportion to the rest of the garment and the size of the wearer.

To achieve the exact lines desired, trace the basic waist or shift sloper onto plain white paper. Some designers prefer marking paper for this purpose because it has crossmarks indicating grain at 1-inch spacing all over the paper. When this pattern is pinned on the dress form, the designer can readily see where yokes, seams, and pockets should be.

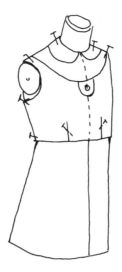

To add style lines to a basic pattern:
1. Cut out paper foundation pattern; both sides of front and back with center front and center back on fold.
2. Close darts and pin on dress form.
3. Draw in desired style lines.
4. Cut out style lines. In case of double thickness, such as pockets, tabs, etc., trace from foundation pattern.
5. Add all seam allowances before cutting in fabric.

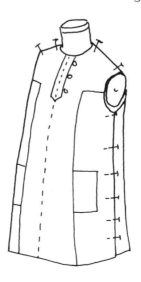

Skirts

Skirts for girls' wear are relatively simple to construct. Girls have very little hip development until they reach Sub-teen sizes, so that there is practically no difference between the waist and hip measurements. In view of the young child's anatomy, and the protruding tummy of the baby stance, the front of the skirt is wider at the waistline than the back. Back measurements, however, increase at the buttock level. Children's skirts, whether they are separate or part of a dress, are usually cut with some sort of fullness for flattery. Gathers, flares, and pleats provide plenty of room for action and give shape to the silhouette of the garment.

THE GATHERED OR DIRNDL SKIRT

This is the most popular skirt for children. It is the simplest to cut. Width is dictated by the design, and often influenced by the width of the fabric. When the fabric is wide enough for the front or the back of the skirt width desired, the skirt is cut in two rectangular pieces joined with side seams.

Example: All-around width desired—80 inches, width of fabric—45 inches

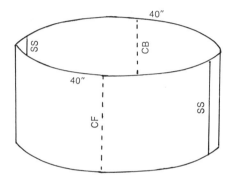

When the fabric is not wide enough to cut the skirt in two pieces, the skirt is cut in three pieces with a seam at each side of the front and at center back. It is usually desirable to avoid a seam at center front.

Example: All-around width desired—80 inches, width of fabric—36 inches

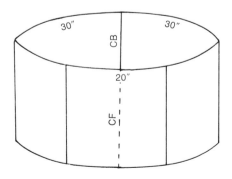

The all-around width (or sweep) of a gathered skirt can range from a relatively narrow 55 inches to a full 105 inches, which is a skirt with three full widths of 36-inch fabric. When full dirndl skirts are in fashion, they are best supported with crisp petticoats to make them stand out.

Since it may be difficult to gather a very full skirt, the fabric may be taken in at the waistline with small overlapping unpressed pleats.

When figuring out the length of the skirt, decide on the finished length, add desired hem + ½ inch for seam allowance at the waistline.

Example:		
Finished length		12″
Hem and turn-in		4½″
Seam allowance at waistline		½″
Cut length of skirt		17″

Straight gathered skirts usually have 3- to 4-inch hems. For sheer party dresses, very deep hems from 5 to 6 inches are used. On the other hand, some manufacturers turning out budget dresses will save fabric and use only 1- to 2-inch hems.

THE FLARED SKIRT

A flared skirt can vary in width from the controlled A-line to the full circle.

The A-line skirt is slightly flared at the sides and mostly suitable for sportswear and tailored dresses. Fabric for this skirt should be firmly woven or backed for shape retention.

To cut an A-line or moderately flared skirt:

    1. Determine waistline measurement and sweep desired.

    2. On a large sheet of paper, draw line for center front.

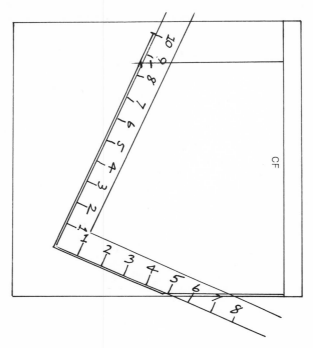

3. Square across one quarter of the waistline measurement; add ¼ inch for A-line, ½ inch for moderately flared skirt.

4. On center front line, measure down the length of the skirt.

5. Square across one eighth of sweep at hem level (one eighth of 40-inch sweep = 5 inches).

6. Place L square so that shorter end rests on the 5-inch mark on the paper, and long end rests against the end of waistline (see illustration).

7. Mark off length of skirt at long end.

8. Reverse L square and square a line down to meet the waistline.

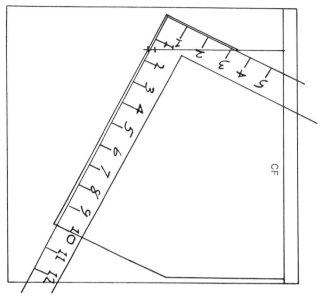

9. Round out waistline and hem as illustrated. Check waistline measurement to make sure that it still equals one quarter of the waist circumference. Make any necessary adjustments by raising or lowering the waistline.

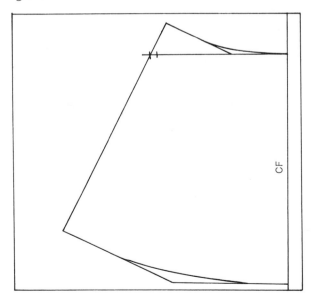

10. To flatten flares at center front, raise waistline approximately ¼ inch as illustrated.

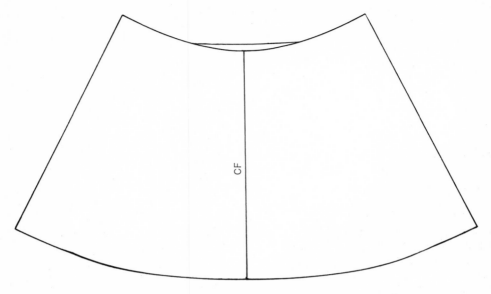

Flared skirts usually have 1- to 2-inch hems, depending on the amount of flare in the skirt. The more circular a skirt becomes, the more difficult it is to handle a deep hem. Therefore even ½-inch hems are not uncommon on full circle skirts.

Once the basic width of the finished skirt has been established, the skirt can be divided into gores as follows:

1. Place skirt pattern on a large flat surface and with a yardstick locate the vanishing point of center front and side seam.

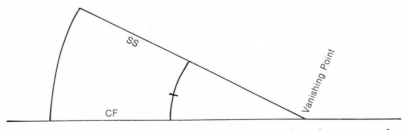

2. On the waistline locate the desired point for placement of gore seam.

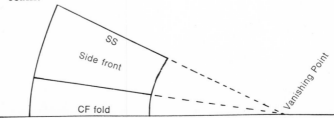

3. Draw gore seam from vanishing point through waistline mark to hem.

This method also makes the proportionate shaping and placement of pockets easy.

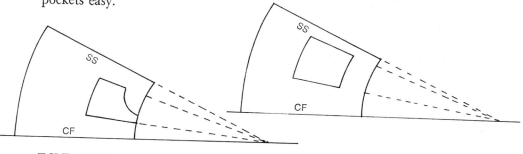

THE FULL CIRCLE SKIRT

A full circle skirt is developed by using a formula to determine the radius of the waistline.

1. The formula is:

$$\frac{WL - 1''}{6} = R$$

Example: Waistline = 22"

$$22'' - 1'' = 21''$$

$$21'' \div 6'' = 3\frac{1}{2}''$$

Radius for waistline = 3½"

2. Draw circle for waistline on paper folded in fourths as illustrated.
3. From waistline measure the desired length. This indicates the hemline.

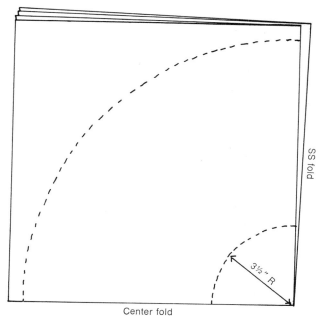

Center fold

PLEATS

Fullness with a more tailored look is achieved with pleats. The fabric is folded and pressed into place, so that the effect is straight and simple when the garment is at rest. In movement, however, there is plenty of fullness and a play of pattern. Following is an analysis of the pleats most often used in children's wear.

Side Pleats—All pleats are pressed to one side, as in the traditional kilt. When pleats are no wider than 1 inch, they are often called *Knife Pleats*.

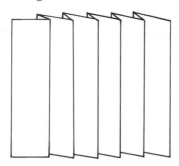

Box Pleats—Pleats are pressed in alternate directions, forming a box.

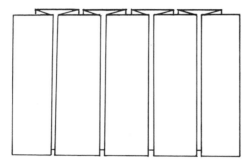

Cluster Pleats—Pleats are folded into clusters and pressed.

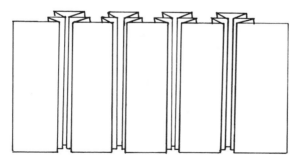

When planning an all-around pleated skirt, a good rule of thumb is to allow three times the waistline measurement for the width of the entire skirt. Each pleat will then lie smoothly at the waistline without bulky overlap. Sometimes lightweight fabrics are planned with deeper pleats, when extra fullness is desired. On the other hand, when manufacturers are cost conscious, they often resort to very shallow pleats. Skimpy pleats usually don't hold their shape, and the results are not satisfactory.

Most sample garments are pleated by the professional pleater. There are, however, rare instances when pressure of time or other considerations require hand pressing. Stock garments are always pleated by the specialist unless the manufacturer has his own pleating plant.

To prepare a skirt for the pleater, join all but one seam and finish the hem. The pleater will want to know the finished width of the waistline, the type of pleating desired, and the width of each pleat. He will plan the pleating pattern, allowing the right amount of underlap for each pleat, and for the older girl (Sub-teen) providing the necessary shaping over the hipline so that the skirt will fall smoothly from waist to hem.

Permanent Pleating, which lasts through many launderings, is achieved by pressing and heating garments made of man-made fibers to just under the melting point of the fiber, and thus molding the fiber to the shape of the pleat. This process is just as effective for textiles consisting of blends of natural and man-made fibers, such as wool and nylon, or cotton and polyester.

Accordion Pleats and Sunburst Pleats both resemble the folds of an accordion.

Accordion Pleats are cut on the straight grain and are the same width throughout. In children's wear, they are used as ruffles or other trimming. Accordion pleats are rarely used for a skirt because they tend to cling too closely to the body for flattery.

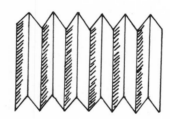

Sunburst Pleats are used to pleat circular skirts. Radiating from the waistline to the hem, they increase in width in proportion to the rest of the skirt.

Both accordion and sunburst pleats are not suitable for hand pressing and are always left to the professional pleater. To prepare a circular skirt for the pleater: join all but one seam; let skirt hang for one or two days so that any necessary adjustments in length can be made to compensate for stretch in the bias grain; finish hem.

Inverted Pleat—Two folds are brought together, often at center front or center back of a garment, to give interest or room for movement.

Inverted pleats, as well as side pleats and box pleats, can be used anywhere in a garment. To make the pattern, fold as desired in paper, and then place the basic pattern over the folded pleats as illustrated.

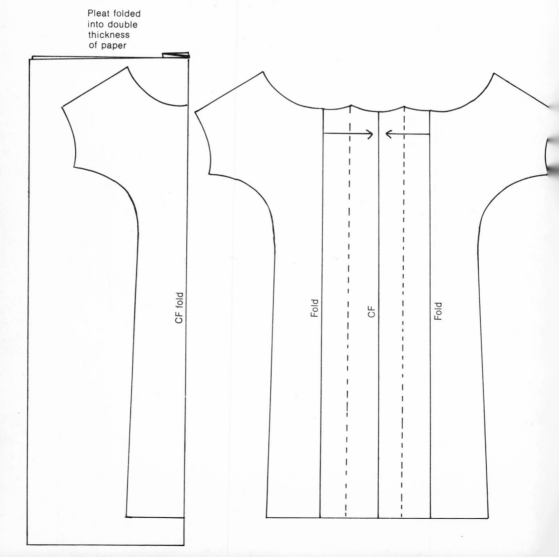

Pleat folded
into double
thickness
of paper

CF fold

Fold

CF

Fold

Pleated Side Panels—Follow the same directions as for inverted pleats. Although pleats pressed by hand will hold their shape better when cut with all creases on grain, it is sometimes preferable to cut pleats deeper at the hemline, following the flare of the skirt.

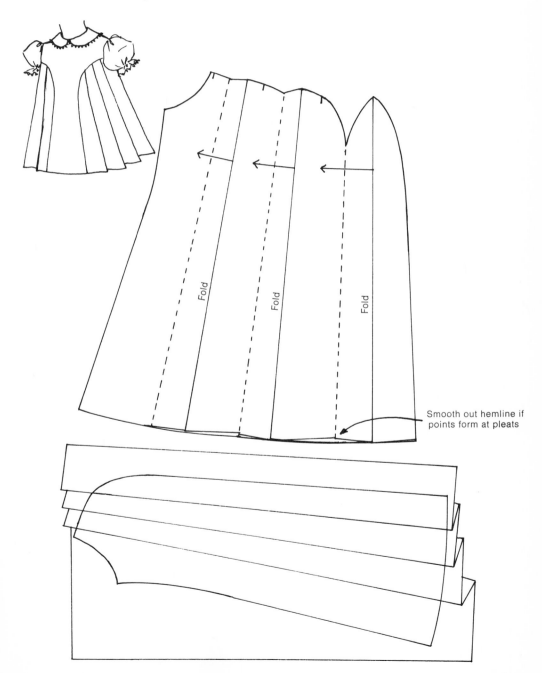

Smooth out hemline if points form at pleats

Slacks

Slacks or trousers in one form or another are worn for all sorts of occasions by most children. Overalls, jeans, and shorts are worn for play. Tailored slacks are worn to school by both girls and boys in many parts of the country. Party slacks, pantsuits, and jumpsuits are made in velvet and other luxurious fabrics for special occasions. Late in the day, children lounge, watch TV, and go to sleep in many types of pajamas.

We shall present here the basic drafting method for slacks patterns. Adjustments for infants' wear, sleepwear, and boys' wear, etc., will be covered in subsequent chapters.

The essential measurements for drafting a slacks pattern are:

1. *Waistline Circumference*
    a. Front—from center front to side seam.
    b. Back—from center back to side seam.

2. *Hip Circumference*
   a. Front—from center front to side seam plus ¼ inch for ease.
   b. Back—from center back to side seam plus ¼ inch for ease.
   Distance from waist to hip level varies according to size range (see Table II). Back hipline measurement is usually wider than front hipline.

3. *Crotch or Seat Level*
   This is the measurement from the waist to the chair when the model is seated. One to 2½ inches of ease, depending on size range and fit desired, are usually added.

4. *Side Seam*
   The measurement from waistline to ankle or top of the shoe, whichever is preferred for the length of the slacks.

5. *Inseam*
   The measurement from the crotch to the ankle or top of shoe. The crotch level should equal the difference between the side-seam and the inseam measurements plus ¼ inch.

Table II—Slacks Measurements for Sample Sizes in Children's Wear

SIZES		2	4	8	10	SUB-TEEN 12
Waist Circumference	Front	5½	6	6¼	6½	6¾
	Back	5	5½	5¾	6	6¼
Hip Circumference	Front	5¾	6¼	7	7¾	8¾
	Back	6	6½	7½	8	9
Distance from Waist to Hip Level		3	3¼	4	4¼	6
Crotch Level (1" Ease)		7	8¼	10½	11¼	11¼
Side Seam		17½	22	32	33¾	36
Inseam		10¾	14	21¾	23	25
Dart Placement	From CB at WL		2½	2⅞	3	3
	Length		3	4⅛	4¼	5

To draft a basic slacks pattern:
   1. On a large piece of paper, draw a vertical guideline.
   2. On this line, mark off waistline, crotch level, and ankle.
   3. Square lines across at waistline, crotch, and ankle.
   4. On crotch line, mark front and back hip-circumference measurements.
   5. Square guidelines up towards waistline for center back and center front.
   6. Place a mark ½ inch in on waistline at center back, and ¼ inch in on waistline at center front.

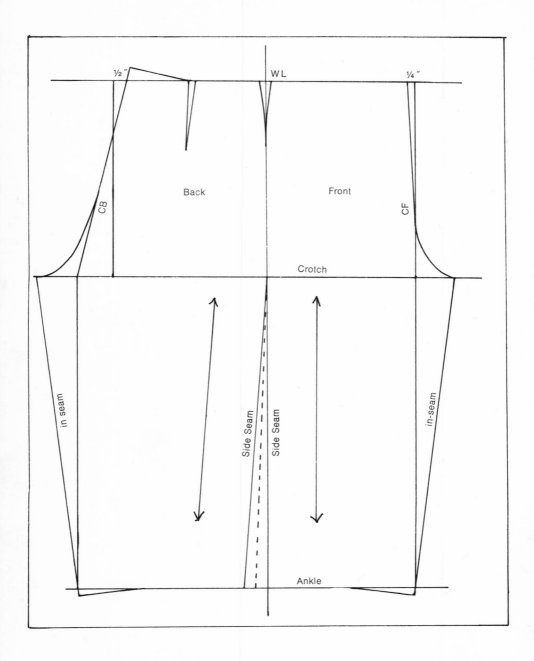

7. Extend one half of back-hip measurement on crotch line.
8. Divide this extension in half, and connect the halfway mark with the point ½ inch in from the center-back guideline at the waistline. Extend line ½ inch above waistline and square toward the waistline as illustrated.
9. Extend one quarter of front-hip measurement on crotch line.
10. Round out both crotch extensions with French curve. Connect center front line to the mark ¼ inch in from the guideline at the waist line.
11. At front, square a guideline from the original hip measurement to the ankle.
12. At back, square a guideline from the halfway mark on the extension to the ankle.
13. Connect inseam line from the extension at front and back to the guideline at the ankle. Square inseam corner toward ankle line.
14. To shape side seam, draw another guideline ½ inch toward back at ankle level, from crotch to ankle. Mark ½ inch at both sides of new guideline for the side seam. This is for classic slacks; for tapered slacks, this measurement is increased. When the side seam is tapered, the inseam must also be tapered for balance.
15. The side seam need not be shaped at the waistline for Toddler sizes. For 3-6x, mark ¼ inch at each side of the side seam at the waistline, and connect to the side seam with the flat end of the French curve. For 7-14 and Sub-teen sizes, mark ½ inch at each side of the waistline, and connect to side seam as above.
16. Establish grain line by squaring a line from the crotch line on front. Match the side seams of both front and back from the crotch line down, and trace the front grain line to the back.
17. Compare the waistline on the pattern with waistline measurements. In most cases there will be no need for any darts at the front. In the back, excess fullness may be shaped in with a dart, or held in with an elastic waistband. For the smaller sizes, the back waist is almost always elasticized for better fit. See Table II for placement and length of the back dart. The direction of the dart should be in harmony with the center-back seam.

Draping in Fabric

The best way to achieve the line of a new fashion is to drape and shape the fabric directly on the dress form. Fabrics vary in texture: some have body and a certain amount of stiffness; others are soft and pliable. By draping, it becomes immediately obvious how much fullness is needed to achieve a certain line or where the precise placement of a styling detail should be.

To drape in fabric:

1. Cut a rectangle of fabric to the approximate dimensions of the particular piece being draped.
    a. Allow fabric for seam allowances, hems, and neckline shaping.
    b. Some facings can be cut in one piece with the garment. Allow approximately 3 inches for facings wherever needed.
    c. Allow enough material for both sides of front or back when there is no seam or closing at center back or center front.
2. Prepare fabric for draping.
    a. Block fabric by pulling grain into straight, perpendicular position. where possible. There is no way of changing the alignment of grain after the finishing process for wash-and-wear or permanent press is completed; therefore these fabrics should be cut as straight as possible, with grain more or less ignored.
    b. Press fabric.
    c. Mark center front and center back with thread or chalk line. Stone chalk, which can be easily removed from the fabric without leaving stains, may be used for marking. Test all fabrics to make sure that no stains remain after removal.
3. Pin center front or center back on dress form. Drape only on one side of the dress form.
4. When draping and pinning are complete, mark seam lines, darts, and pleats, etc., with chalk or pins and remove from dress form.
5. True all lines by connecting chalk marks or pins with thread tracing or chalk lines. Some designers merely add accurate seam allowances and cut out. To do this, one must be sure that all markings are perfect.

6. Fold on center and cut out other side, transferring any necessary markings with pins and chalk.
7. For future reference, cut paper pattern of draped garment before it is sewn together.

Chapter 7 / *Special Problems*

Infants' Wear

CLOTHING for children during the first year of life must meet many unique requirements. Infants need body coverings that protect against extremes in temperature without causing discomfort. It is essential that all garments be easily washable at high temperature and need little or no ironing. Openings should be large enough so that frequent changes don't create too much fuss for mother and baby. Since the infant's skin is sensitive, fabrics used for his clothing should always be soft and non-irritating. For example, scratchy organdy or coarse wool is most unsuitable. The most widely used fabrics for infants' wear are cotton knits or blends of cotton and polyester, either knitted or woven, but always finished so that the fabric is soft to the touch. Modern child experts agree that, for optimum development of the infant, clothing should be constructed so that it is not restrictive. There should be plenty of room for movement, but garments should not be so large that they cause uncomfortable folds and bunches. Certain safety factors must also be considered in designing infants' wear. Using drawstrings around the neck for fastening is a hazard. So is the use of buttons that could be pulled off and swallowed. Instead, gripper fasteners or soft nylon zippers provide safe and efficient closings. In view of the rapid development of the infant, many garments are outgrown both physically and functionally in a relatively short time. Stretch fabrics provide room for growth and extend the use of some garments. Nevertheless, the baby's first wardrobe, the layette, may be outgrown within the first three months of life. For most babies, the layette is kept simple and includes only the bare necessities for the first few months.

Basic layettes consist of:

Gowns and kimonos or wrappers—These are the garments worn for sleeping, the activity infants are engaged in 80 percent of the time during the first few months of life. Gowns are long garments with a placket opening at the neck and a drawstring or envelope fold at the bottom. Their main advantage is that they keep baby's feet warm during cold weather. Kimonos or wrappers are also cut long, but they open all the way down the front and are easier to get in

167

and out of. Many kimonos are cut with raglan sleeves, a style which provides a comfortable armhole and seems to fit for a longer period of time than the regular set-in sleeve.

The following table gives the garment measurements for Infants' size gowns and wrappers as recommended by the United States Department of Commerce. These measurements were developed for gowns and wrappers of flat knit cotton fabric.

Table III

SIZE		6 MO	12 MO.
Width of garment	(C-D)	12	12½
Total length:	(A-B)		
Gowns		28	30
Wrappers		21	23
End of sleeve to end of			
sleeve across garment:	(G-H)		
Open sleeve		26	28
Closed sleeve		30	32
Short sleeve		18	19½
Width at bottom:	(K-L)		
Gowns		19	20
Wrappers		16	17
Neck opening		10	10½
Opened up		18	19
Armhole length	(F-N)	5½	5½

Method of Measuring

Width of garment—Measured across the garment 1 inch below the bottom of the armholes.

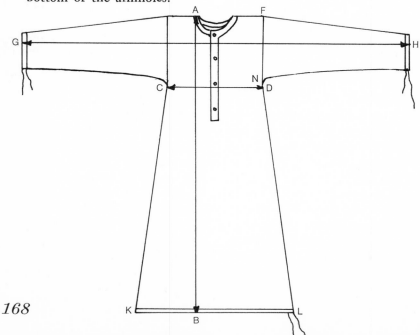

Total length—Measured from the point where the shoulder meets the
neck opening to the bottom of the garment.

End of sleeve to end of sleeve across garment—With the neck fastening
closed and each sleeve fully extended as the garment lies flat, the

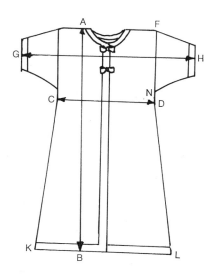

measurement is taken from the outer end of one sleeve across the
body of the garment to the outer end of the other sleeve.

Width at bottom—Measured between the outside edges of the extreme
bottom of the garment.

Neck opening—With neck fastening closed, measure the circumference
of the neck at the top edge, with fabric relaxed and smooth.

Armhole length—Measured from the point where the sleeve is attached
to the shoulder to the lowest point under the arm.

Shirts—There are several types of baby shirts. For cold climates, there
are double-breasted shirts that either snap or tie at the sides. Some
mothers prefer shirts that slip over the head. These shirts have adjustable necklines and no fastenings to fuss with. For warm weather,
there are sleeveless shirts with built-up straps over the shoulders. All
shirts are made of cotton knit for comfort and absorbency. Diaper
tabs, to which the diaper is pinned, are sewn inside the shirt at
each side. They keep the shirt from getting wet and prevent pin
holes, which develop when the diaper is pinned directly to the shirt.

The following table gives the garment measurements for infants' and
children's shirts as recommended by the United States Department of
Commerce. These measurements were developed for shirts of ribbed
(1x1) knit cotton.

Table IV

SIZE		3 MO.	6 MO.	12 MO.	18 MO.	24 MO.	36 MO.
Width of garment:	(C-D)						
Sleeves		7	7½	7½	8	8½	9
Sleeveless		6½	7	7	7½	8	8½
Total length	(A-B)	10	11	12	14	16	17
Sleeve length:	(E-F)						
Long		7	7½	8	9	10	11
Short		2¾	3	3½	3¾	3¾	4
Armhole length:	(G-E)						
Sleeves		4	4¼	4½	4¾	5	5¼
Sleeveless		4¼	4½	4¾	5	5½	5¾
Neck opening:							
Flat		9½	10	10½	11	11½	12
Stretched		17½	18	19	19½	20	20½
Sleeveless shirt		16½	17¼	18	18¾	19½	20¼
Sleeveless shirt:							
Shoulder-strap length	(H-I)	2¾	3	3¼	3½	3¾	4
Shoulder-strap width		1¼	1¼	1¼	1¼	1¼	1¼

Method of measuring

Width of garment—Measured across the garment 1″ below the bottom
of the armhole.

Total length—Measured from the point where the shoulder joins the
collarette or neck opening to the bottom of the shirt.

Sleeve length—Measured in a straight line from the point under the
arm where the sleeve is seamed to the garment to the lower outer
edge of the sleeve, or sleeve cuff, if a cuff is used.

Armhole length—Measured from the point where the sleeve is attached
to the shoulder to the lowest point under the arm.

Neck opening—pullover styles:

flat—measured by taking the circumference at the top edge with the
fabric relaxed and smooth.

stretched—measured by taking the circumference of the neck at the
seam, with the fabric stretched.

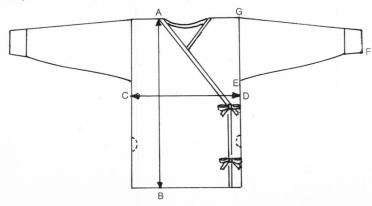

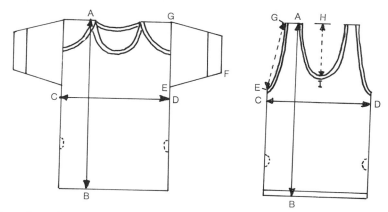

Sleeveless shirt—shoulder strap:
  shoulder-strap length—measured from the point where the shoulder
    strap joins the body of the garment to the top edge of the strap.
  shoulder-strap width—measured across the strap at the top edge of
    the strap.

Diapers—Washable, rectangular diapers come in various weaves of
  cotton material. Gauze and birdseye are the most popular. Recently,
  however, many mothers have come to prefer disposable diapers.
  These have been improved so that they are very absorbent and comfortable. Disposable diapers have a waterproof covering so that the
  need for diaper pants is eliminated.

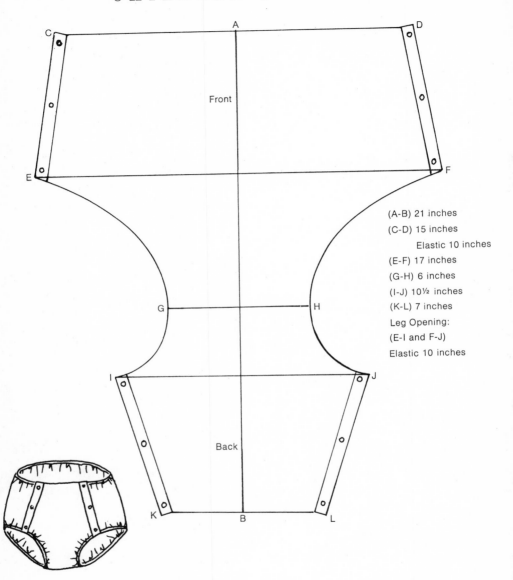

Front

Back

(A-B) 21 inches
(C-D) 15 inches
Elastic 10 inches
(E-F) 17 inches
(G-H) 6 inches
(I-J) 10½ inches
(K-L) 7 inches
Leg Opening:
(E-I and F-J)
Elastic 10 inches

Diaper pants—When washable diapers are used, a waterproof covering is needed to protect bedding and other clothing. Plastic or rubber pants serve this purpose. Some diaper pants are made of knitted or woven fabric and lined with plastic. They are usually fastened with grippers at the sides so that they open flat for easy changes.

Sweaters and hats—These are needed for outdoor use. Knitted or crocheted of nylon, acrylic, or cotton, they should be washable, warm, and non-irritating to the baby's skin.

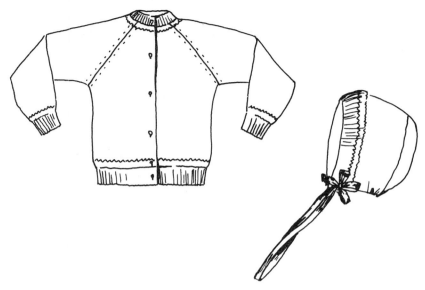

Bibs—Bibs are needed to protect baby's clothing at feeding time, and later when the baby is teething, to absorb some of the moisture from drooling. They are usually designed in some soft absorbent fabric, such as terrycloth or several layers of gauze, and backed with plastic.

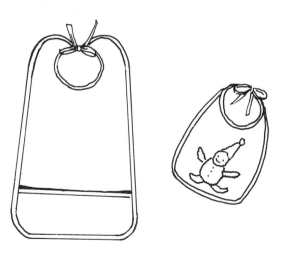

To complete the baby's layette, baby blankets, crib sheets, and pads are needed. Although these items don't necessarily fall into the category of clothing, they are often manufactured by the same firms that produce the shirts, the gowns, and the kimonos. Several large infants' wear firms produce all the above items except the diapers, which are manufactured by specialists. The designs for layette garments are fairly standard, placing emphasis on comfort and function. Modifications are usually the result of some new development in textiles or construction, which increases comfort for baby or reduces work for mother. Nevertheless, designers add appeal to layettes by working out color-coordinated groups and presenting them in attractive packages. Delicate prints are often used for wrappers and gowns. Dainty or colorful stitching or embroidery are used for trimmings rather than bunchy ruffles. A good sense of proportion is essential when designing these tiny garments. Very little else is needed to make them attractive and appealing to the consumer.

After the first few months, when the baby is awake for longer periods of time and becomes more active, his clothing requirements increase. Mother usually likes to dress him up for company and for his daily outings, and more items are likely to be added to his wardrobe. Since these garments are often purchased as gifts, they are designed to be appealing as well as practical.

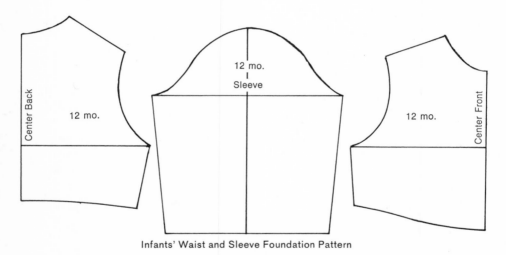

Infants' Waist and Sleeve Foundation Pattern

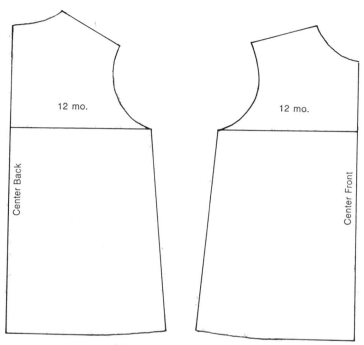

Infants' Shift Foundation Pattern

Sample size in this group is usually 12 months. Although body measurements are included in the Appendix, the foundation pattern is most easily developed on the dress form (see page 292). It is advisable to work with a full-length dress form when designing for infants, because it gives a somewhat better concept of the proportions of the infant's body. This is, however, no substitute for the actual child, because a rigid form cannot approximate the posture and flexibility of the baby. It must be remembered that, for practical reasons, the legs of the dress form must be straight, whereas the child's legs are always bent at the knees before he learns to walk. The form is upright, suspended from a stand, but the baby must be visualized lying or sitting in the crib, playpen, baby seat, or carriage. The body shape of the infant eliminates the need for any darts. Although a waistline level is indicated with a tape on the dress form, it is mainly useful for locating the upper edge of trousers. When designing dresses or toppers for infants, if a waistline is desired, it is arbitrarily placed to suit the proportions of the finished garment.

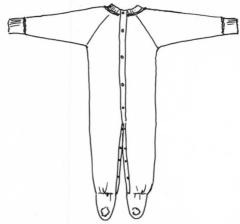

Additional clothing for the first year includes:

Coverall stretch suits—These knit suits cover baby from neck to toe and stretch a size or two so that they are comfortable and non-restricting. They keep the infant covered without being bulky, and snap open down the front and along the legs so that changing diapers is no problem. As a rule, they are knitted of 100 percent nylon or a blend of cotton and nylon.

Topper sets—Some manufacturers refer to these popular outfits for boys and girls as diaper sets. In any case, they consist of a panty, sometimes lined with plastic so that it serves as a diaper cover, and matching top. For boys there are matching tailored shirts, and for girls there are more feminine tops. Embroidery, appliqué, and lace edgings are used for trimming, and the fabrics vary but should meet the requirements for easy washability and comfort for the baby. There are many variations on the topper set. For cool weather, toppers are sold with matching nylon stretch tights. Another version is the completely knitted outfit for outdoors, consisting of leggings with feet, sweater, and hat. In summer, the topper set is often a sunsuit with a matching cover-up.

Crawlers—For the second half of the first year, the crawler becomes an important item in the baby's wardrobe. The classic crawler is pants with gripper fasteners along the crotch, held up with straps that button to a built-up front. These are usually worn with a long- or short-sleeved polo shirt. Sometimes crawlers are designed as a coverall, a one-piece garment with sleeves and collar. Fabrics for crawlers should be sturdy: denim or other firm cottons for summer and corduroy for winter. Three-piece sets, consisting of crawler with matching jacket and hat, are popular for spring and fall outdoor wear.

To draft a basic slacks pattern, see page 161. The side seam may be eliminated in infants' wear to simplify construction. The measurements necessary to draft the size 12 month crawler pattern are:

Side seam	15″
Inseam	8¾″
Crotch level or true rise	6¼″
Hip circumference	21″
Hip-front measurement	5¼″
Hip-back measurement	5¼″

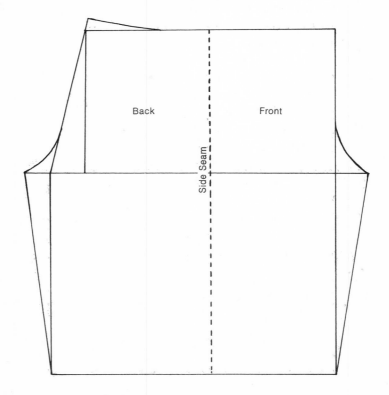

For a one-piece coverall or to design a crawler with built-up front and back sections:

1. Establish side seam on crawler pattern so that the front waistline measures 5½ inches and the back waistline measures 5 inches. This corresponds with the waistline on the front and back waist pattern.
2. Separate front and back of the crawler pattern.
3. Place the front and back waist patterns so that the waistlines of the crawler and the top meet at the center front. There will be a

space at the side seam and center back between the pants and waist patterns. See page 233 for Basic Jumpsuit Pattern.

4. Draw in any desired style lines.

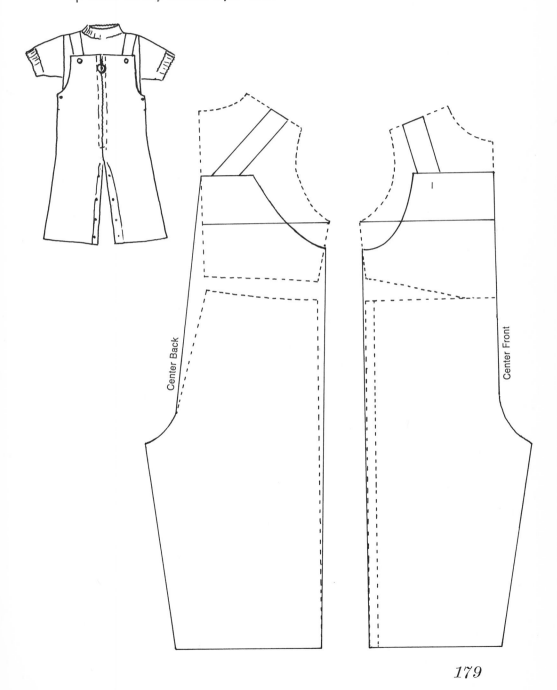

Center Back

Center Front

Pram bags, buntings, and pram suits—For really cold winter weather, the baby needs a warm outfit for his carriage rides. Pram bags are easiest to get in and out of. They are loose bag-like coverings fitted with sleeves that cover the hands, and a hood. Buntings come in two or three pieces: a jacket with a separate or attached hood, and a simple blanket bag which covers the baby up

to the chest and shoulders. The pram suit is mostly sold for babies in the second half of their first year. It is a one-piece coverall-type garment with attached feet and a matching hat or hood. Fabrics for these outfits vary, but they are always warm, lightweight, and washable. Nylons, polyester and cotton blends, and corduroy, together with acrylic pile or quilted linings, are usually used.

Blanket sleepers or pajama blankets—These are warm, coverall garments of blanket fabric, usually a brushed acrylic, that is soft and washable. As the baby gets older and tends to kick off his covers, these blanket suits keep him warm all through the night. They are usually designed with a zipper that opens from neck to crotch and along the leg to facilitate diaper changes.

The luxuries—Beyond the necessities for an infant's wardrobe, there is a good market in out-and-out luxury items for the baby. These are rarely purchased by the mother, but are often irresistible to grandparents and other doting friends and relatives when selecting gifts. Among these luxury garments are dresses and sweaters lavish with hand stitching and embroidery. Important in this category are elaborate long christening dresses embellished with exquisite laces and other delicate trimming. The fabric for these dresses is

almost always the finest silky cotton batiste. Hand-knit sweaters are still fashioned from very fine soft wool, although acrylic yarns are also used because of their non-allergic and easy-care properties. These special garments cannot be mass produced and are usually imported from other countries, such as France, Switzerland, Italy, and the Philippines, where skilled hand labor is still available. Some American manufacturers design these garments in the United States, but use production facilities in other countries.

Sportswear

There is more sportswear sold than any other kind of children's apparel. Sportswear is worn for all occasions. In school, at play, and even for parties we see children wearing separates that are produced by sportswear manufacturers. One reason for the popularity of sportswear for children is that separates fit for a longer period of time than one-piece garments. The separation at the waistline allows for growth. Another advantage is that skirts, slacks, blouses, sweaters, and jackets can be mixed and matched in any number of combinations, creating a variety of outfits.

Every year, the typical children's sportswear house manufactures three seasonal collections of separates for all occasions. The Fall line consists of outfits for school wear. Blouses, shirts, sweaters, and jackets are teamed with skirts, jumpers, and slacks in coordinated fabrics. Acrylics, blends of wool with acrylics or nylon, cotton corduroy, and other sturdy cottons are traditional fall fabrics. For blouses and shirts, blends of cotton and polyester are most commonly used.

The Holiday line is more dressy, with velveteen separates, frilly blouses, and a generally softer look. Skating skirts and tops are also included in many collections at this time. These, along with sweaters and blouses, are popular gift items. The selling season is short but intensive before Christmas, and for children's sportswear this is a very lively season.

On the other hand, the selling season for Spring and Summer sportswear merchandise is a long one. A preliminary group of summer things has already been included in the Holiday line for resort- or cruise-wear selling. As family weekend vacations occur throughout the year and indoor swimming pools are featured at most resort hotels, there is a constant market for bathing suits and cover-ups. Also, family winter holidays in the tropics are not as rare as they used to be, and of course, the children who live in Florida or Southern California need summer sportswear the year around. Consequently, spring and summer separates are sold in most stores from November to July. For only a few months, starting in mid-

August, do most children's sportswear departments limit their stocks to wintry merchandise. Spring and summer sportswear consists of shorts, slacks, skirts, and tops of light, bright fabrics. Tennis dresses and bathing suits are included in some lines. Most of the bathing suits, however, are manufactured by the large swimsuit houses that produce swimwear for adults as well as children. In addition, children's knitwear manufacturers also produce bathing suits for summer selling. Fabrics for warm-weather sportswear are mostly cottons, or blends of cotton and polyester for easy washing with no ironing.

Most styles for girls' sportswear are cut from size 3, or 4, to 14. Garments are cut in sizes 4-6x at one price, and in sizes 7-14 at a slightly higher price to cover the additional fabric requirements. Size 3 is often eliminated from the smaller range, because typical separates do not seem to work for the child who is smaller than a size 4. Therefore, Toddler sportswear is usually cut in sizes 2T-4T. On the other end of the size scale are the Sub-teens, sizes 6-14, with their own more sophisticated styling.

SEPARATES

Following is an analysis of the special problems of which a designer must be aware when creating the various items included in a sportswear collection.

Blouses and Shirts

Blouses are soft and dressy. Shirts are tailored. Blouses fit the same way as a dress around the shoulders and armholes, whereas shirts may have a straighter armhole and a flattened-cap-type sleeve. Although blouses may be styled to look neat and tailored, they usually are trimmed with ruffles, lace, or fancy stitching. On the other hand, shirts may also have frills for trimming, but they usually have tailored design features such as back yokes, two-piece shirt collars, long sleeves with cuffs, pockets, and double-needle stitching.

Adjustment of the Basic Pattern for a Blouse

1. Add 5 to 7 inches (depending on size) below the waistline at the side seam.
2. Square a line from center front and center back for lowered hem of blouse.
3. Square a line up from the hemline to the intersection of the armhole and side seam.
4. If desired, shape the new side seam, as illustrated, to eliminate some of the waistline fullness.
5. Add extension and facing at center front.

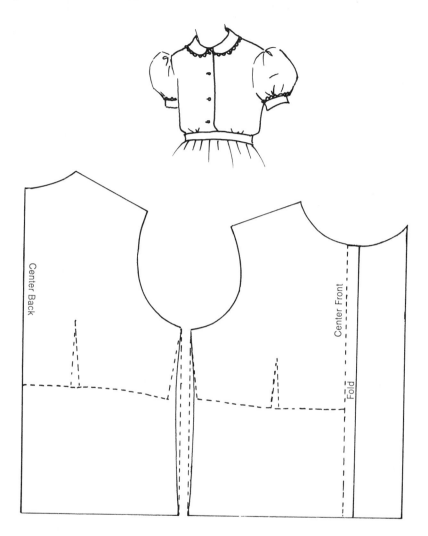

Adjustment of the Basic Pattern for a Shirt

1. Straighten and lower the armhole as illustrated. Lower the armhole to the extent that the straightened armhole remains the same size as the original armhole.
2. Lower the waistline and shape the side seam the same as for the blouse.
3. Add extension and facing at center front.
4. Flatten the cap of the Basic Sleeve (see Shirtwaist Sleeve, page 115).
5. Measure the sleeve cap. The cap should not be more than ½ inch longer than the armhole.

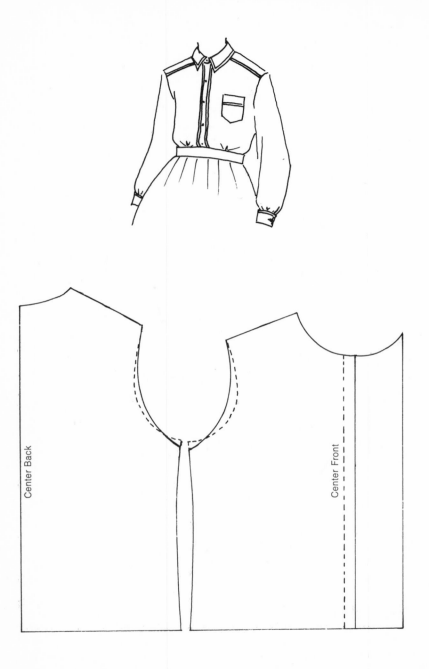

Special Problems

Blouse-slips

Blouse-slips combine the blouse or shirt with a petticoat. They are particularly useful for active little girls who have difficulty in keeping their blouses tucked neatly inside their skirts. Blouse-slips may be manufactured by blouse specialists or by the firms producing slips and underwear. The pattern for a blouse-slip may be based on a basic waist foundation with a flared skirt, or on the basic shift. Ruffles or lace edging usually substitute for a hem.

Skirts

Separate skirts for children may be pleated, gathered, or flared. For the toddler, skirts must be suspended from the shoulders with straps or buttoned to the waist of the blouse, because the very young child's body has not enough shape to hold up a skirt at the waistline. Older girls manage very nicely with a waistband, especially when the waistband is elasticized at the back, so that it can adjust to individual differences of waistline measurements. To cut gathered, flared, and pleated skirts, see pages 147-157.

To cut a waistband for a skirt:

1. Measure the waistline and add ½ inch for ease.

Back   Front

Side Seam   Fold   Side Seam

2. Add 1-inch underlap at placket as illustrated.

Special elastic for children's waistbands is 1 inch wide, soft, and has a great amount of stretch. It may be sewn in at the center back of the waistband or in two sections, at each side back.

Jumpers

Jumpers are sleeveless garments designed to be worn over blouses or sweaters. There are many reasons for their popularity in all size ranges. Blouses stay neatly in place regardless of how active the child is. In cold

climates, they add extra warmth. Since there is no need for a waistband, they are often more comfortable than a skirt. Jumpers can be styled in many ways. They may have a waistline at the normal, empire, or lowered level. They can be fitted with princess seams or cut like a shift. There is really no end to the possible varieties of jumpers. Fabrics can range from the familiar blue serge of the school uniform to bright cottons, corduroy, or velveteen. Almost anything is suitable except sheer fabrics. Since the jumper must fit over a blouse or a sweater, the foundation pattern must be adjusted. The amount of adjustment is dependent on the weight of the fabric of the jumper and the type of garment over which it is to be worn. For example, the adjustment of the pattern for a cotton jumper to be

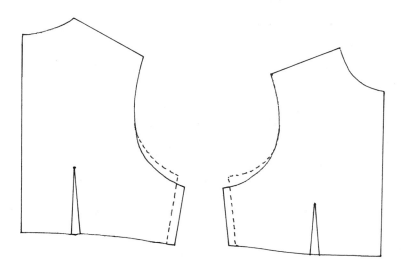

worn over a sheer blouse is not as great as the adjustment for a wool tweed jumper to be worn with a sweater.

Average Adjustment of the Basic Pattern for a Jumper:

1. Lower the armhole ½ inch.
2. Extend the side seam ¼ inch.

Slacks, Shorts, and Culottes

Trousers are worn by both boys and girls of all ages year in and year out. Occasionally, fashion changes require the development of new patterns to conform to the current silhouette. Slacks may taper close to the leg, hang straight from the hips, or flare out from the knee. They can vary in length from very short shorts to any point above or below the knee, depending on the fashionable length of the season.

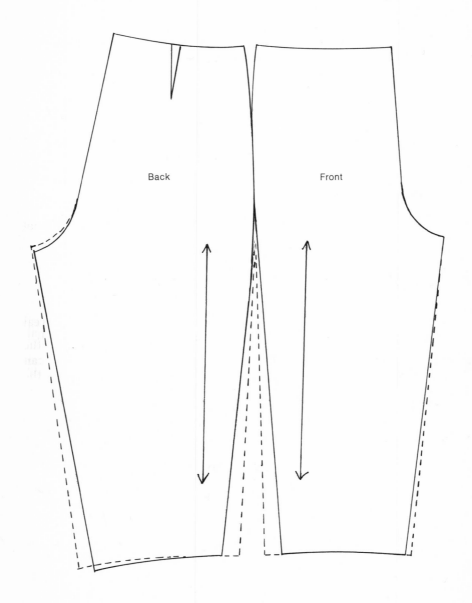

Back

Front

To taper slacks:

It is best to taper slacks by adjusting the basic pattern on the slacks form and taking in the desired amount at the side seam and the inseam. When slacks are very tapered and fitted to the buttocks, the back of the crotch must be lowered, raising the grain along the back inseam and in this way taking more fullness from the back of the slacks leg than the front.

Adjustment of the basic slacks pattern for moderately tapered slacks, when a slacks form is not available:

1. Lower the back crotch ½ inch for size 10, ¼ inch for size 4.
2. Taper the side seam, beginning just above the crotch level, to 1¼ inches at the ankle for size 10, ¾ inch for size 4.
3. Taper the back inseam, beginning at the crotch level, to 1¼ inches at the ankle for size 10, ¾ inch for size 4.
4. Lengthen the back inseam ½ inch for size 10, ¼ inch for size 4.
5. Taper the front inseam ¼ inch at the ankle for all sizes.

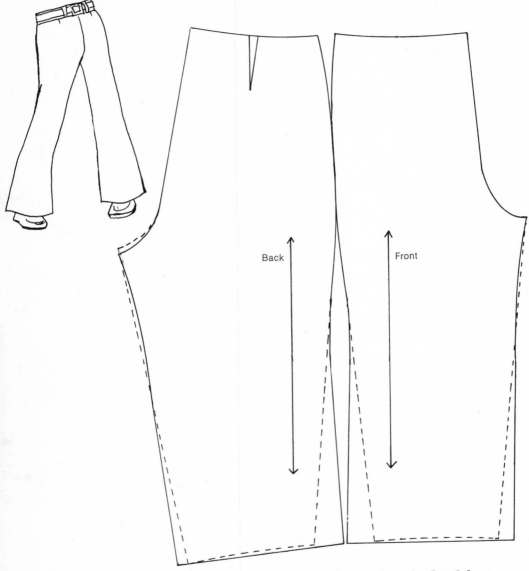

Adjustment of the tapered slacks pattern for moderately flared lower leg:

1. Lower the back crotch another ½ inch for size 10, ¼ inch for size 4.
2. Bring the back inseam in another ¼ inch at the ankle.
3. Beginning at the knee level, add desired amount of flare. For moderate flare, add 2 inches at the side seam for size 10, 1¼ inch for size 4. Add 1 inch at the inseam for size 10, ¾ inch for size 4.

Special Problems

Adjustment of the basic slacks pattern for jeans (tapered or flared pattern may also be used):

1. Mark off the shape of the yoke below the waistline on the back pattern.
2. To eliminate the back dart, slash the pattern on the yoke line from the side seam to the dart. Close the dart in the yoke area. When the dart extends into the lower part of the pattern, take off the necessary amount at the center-back seam as illustrated.
3. Mark off the pocket opening on the front pattern.
4. Indicate the shape of the inside pocket.
5. Add the placket for the fly front to the center-front seam. The placket may be cut in one with the front or separately. For an inexpensive method of construction, see Boys' Wear, page 240.

Back

Front

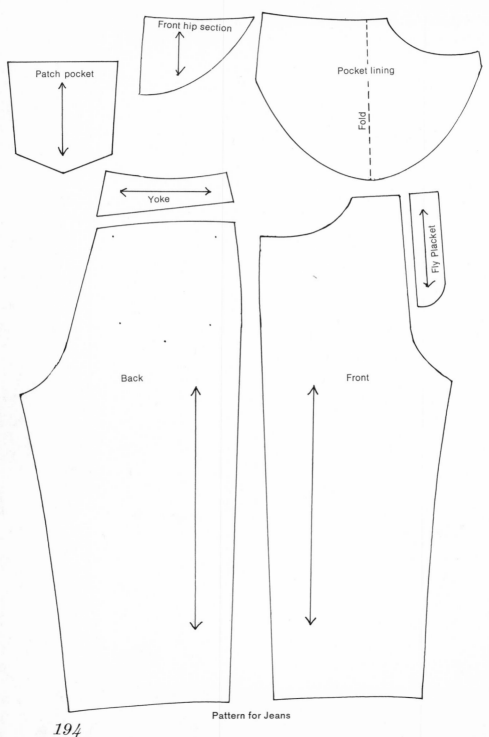

Patch pocket

Front hip section

Pocket lining

Fold

Yoke

Fly Placket

Back

Front

Pattern for Jeans

Special Problems

Adjustment of the basic slacks pattern for shorts:

1. Cut off at desired length.
2. Add hem or facing.

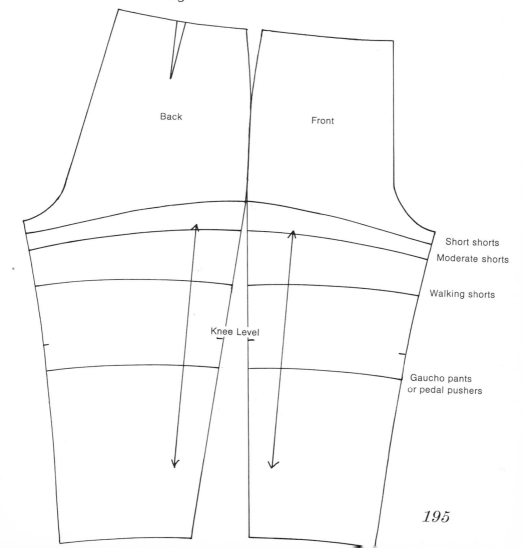

Back

Front

Short shorts

Moderate shorts

Walking shorts

Knee Level

Gaucho pants
or pedal pushers

Adjustment of the basic slacks pattern for culottes:

1. Construct desired skirt pattern. See page 198.
2. Superimpose the crotch seam area from the basic slacks pattern at the center-front and the center-back seams of the skirt.
3. Draw the inseam of the culottes parallel to the center-front and the center-back seams of the skirt.

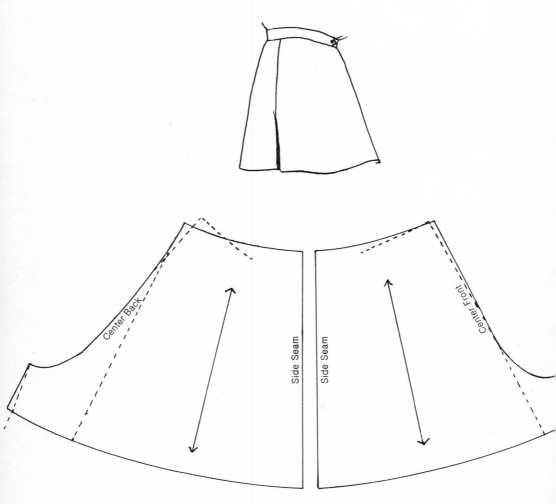

Pattern for flared culottes

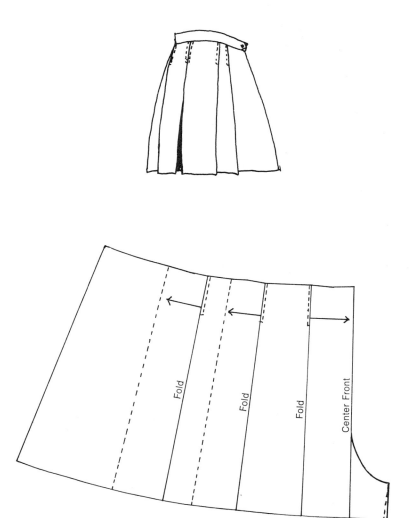

Pattern for front of Pleated Culottes

Jackets

A jacket may be designed as a unit in a group of coordinates or in combination with a specific skirt and blouse, to form a suit. A jacket may also be designed to be worn with a dress as an ensemble. Since jackets usually must fit over another garment, the foundation pattern should be adjusted.

Average adjustment of the basic pattern for a jacket:
1. Lower the neckline ⅛ inch all around.
2. Raise the shoulder ⅛ inch at the armhole.
3. Extend the shoulder ⅛ inch at the armhole.
4. Lower the armhole ¼ inch.
5. Extend the side seam ¼ inch.
6. Slash the sleeve as illustrated. Spread ¼ inch at the vertical slashes and ⅛ inch at the horizontal slashes.

These measurements may be varied according to the type of fabric used or the purpose of the jacket. For example: the pattern for lined jackets of heavy fabrics will need more adjustment than the pattern for unlined cotton jackets. The foundation pattern, to be used for a jacket or a cover-up designed to be worn over a sundress or a bathing suit, may need no adjustment at all.

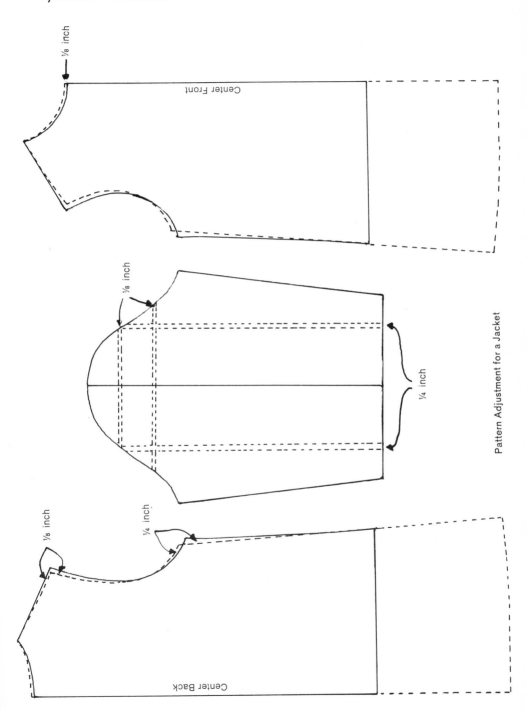

⅛ inch

Center Front

⅛ inch

Pattern Adjustment for a Jacket

¼ inch

⅛ inch

¼ inch

Center Back

SWEATERS

The job of designing sweaters is unique in that the designer works from scratch, determining not only the cut and trimming of the garment, but also creating the actual fabric. Just as for the designer of textiles, the first thing in designing a collection of sweaters must be the shopping of the yarn market to select colors and various textured yarns to be knitted into garments. The designer selects the colors and the types of yarn that will be used for the collection. The next step is to determine which stitches will be fashionable and will create the desired effects. The possibilities for surface interest in knitted fabrics are endless. In addition to simple flat effects, ribs, cables, openwork, and endless jacquard designs are possible. The term "jacquard" is used in knitting to include not only patterns using various colored yarns, but also patterns created by intricate stitching repeats. Technicians, rather than designers, handle the knitting machines and work out samples from the designer's diagrams. The manufacturers of knitting machinery maintain large libraries of swatches, illustrating the design potential of their machines. Most fashion designers use these samples freely. Beginning with a swatch of fancy stitching, they develop a "new" fabric in fashionable colors and the weight that is currently desirable. There are usually several samples knitted before the designer gets exactly the fabric that she wants. The weight of the yarn, the tension of the stitch, and the combination of colors all influence the end result.

Sweaters and other knitted garments can be roughly divided into two categories: fully fashioned and cut-and-sew. Fully fashioned sweaters or dresses are knitted to the shape of each individual pattern piece and then sewn together, whereas the cut-and-sew method involves cutting the garment pieces from knitted fabric, and then sewing them together. The development of the overedge machine, which firmly overcasts the cut edge of each pattern piece as seams are being stitched, has made the cut-and-sew method practical. Without this secure method of locking in the edges of each cut piece, there is the likelihood that the garment will unravel. Most large firms use both methods of production to achieve varying effects. Fully fashioned sweaters are usually somewhat costly to produce. Consequently, the large bulk of American knitwear is cut out from knitted fabric, which has been either finished flat like woven yard goods or knitted in tubular shape. Almost all knitting machines produce yard goods in a circular fashion, producing a tube of fabric which is pressed flat and rolled for shipping. When knit garments are cut from yard goods which have been finished so that they retain their shape in handling and wear, the methods of production are not much different from those used in manufacturing apparel from woven fabrics. Therefore, many general sportswear and dress manufacturers are also producing sweaters and other knit garments. It must be said, however, that manufacturers specializing in sweaters have the various machines required for the smooth finishing of necklines and closings, and usually produce a better finished product.

SWIMWEAR

Sometime in March, usually after a good vacation, the children's swim-wear designer begins work on a new collection. This collection will reach its peak selling season in the retail stores a year and a half later. In contrast to other children's wear areas, there is only one collection every year. Its selling season in the wholesale market extends through several seasons. The first group of samples must be ready in June, when the mail-order houses place orders for next year's summer catalogues. Specialty shops and department stores buy swimsuits for cruise-wear selling in late August and early September. Then in January the complete line is shown and the bulk of the business is placed for summer selling. Fill-in orders and re-orders continue well into spring while the design room is busy with next year's models. This is the tempo of swimwear, an area that has many unique problems and demands an extraordinary amount of expertise from the designer.

Special Problems

Most swimwear designers cut their own samples. Sketches can only give a rough approximation of a finished swimsuit. The stretch and general behavior of the fabric will affect the proportions of the suit, and each design is a three-dimensional problem that must be carefully worked out. The designer and the patternmaker usually work together to develop the foundation pattern for each type of fabric. Although a full-length leg form is used in the design room, all new patterns must be tested on a child before they go into production. The amount and direction of the stretch in fabric, the type and amount of elastic used in a cotton suit, and the general silhouette of the suit all affect the fit and function of the garment and must be tested. Ideally, the swimsuit should not only be tested for fit in the design room but under the conditions of normal use, immersed in the swimming pool and the ocean.

The sample room of a swimsuit house is equipped with the machines necessary to turn out a sample that is finished just like a stock garment. Special overedge and elastic-covering machines as well as many attachments are available to turn out a professional product.

Designing swimwear is probably the most challenging of all the specialties in children's wear design. The function of swimwear imposes a number of very rigid limitations within which the designer must work and still produce a new and fresh line year after year. First of all, swimsuits are most definitely active sportswear. Swimsuits must move with the child and be completely non-restrictive, while at the same time they must hug the body without irritating or binding in any way.

The fabrics used for swimsuits must meet very rigid specifications. Colors must be impervious to sun, salt, and chlorine. Children's swimsuits are not only used for swimming, but they must take constant abuse from active play in the sand as well as on the playground. When the suit is taken off, it usually goes into the washer and the dryer so that it will be clean and ready for another round of water, sand, and sun on the next day. Certain colors and weaves can't take this sort of endless harsh wear. The designer must limit her choices to the fabrics that can. Nylon, with its great strength, stretchability, and quick-drying property is an excellent choice, and stretch-knit nylon has become a classic for swimsuits. Woven cottons that are completely colorfast are somewhat less expensive to use. Most swimsuits need linings; when they are used, they must be carefully chosen so that they work well with the outer fabric. Nylon tricot is usually used inside a 100 percent stretch nylon suit, whereas cotton batiste may be used to line a cotton suit.

When designing a bathing suit, the designer must work within a very small area. Working out the right proportions sometimes poses a special problem. Toddlers and pre-school children tend to look appealing in most bathing suits, and sub-teens with their developing young bodies are not particularly difficult to design for. The 7-14 girl, however, is the real problem here. Her taste often demands a grown-up look, but her figure hasn't achieved the right curves as yet. Her tummy still protrudes more than her chest and it is difficult to make her look as curvacious as her older sister. At the same time, the 7-14 girl is an avid swimmer and needs suits that really function well in the water, suits that stay in place during all sorts of active swimming and diving. For this sort of activity, a tank suit with its built-up shoulder straps always works well, and designers must try to do something new with the tank suit every season. But functional tank suits aren't the complete answer to the 7-14 swimsuit problem. Most schoolgirls are very fashion conscious and like to adopt the ideas that are popular for the sub-teen and junior market. Bikinis, swim dresses, rompers —if it's in for juniors it has to be worked out proportionally so that it also looks well on the 7-14 girl.

Most designers create two kinds of swimsuits, those used primarily for actual swimming and those that function as a playsuit as well. Both are needed by most children who spend their summers at the shore or in the country. Even the average youngster, living in a suburban house with a plastic pool in the backyard, wears swimsuits all day long. When one suit is wet, a child will change into another one. The swimsuit that also doubles as a playsuit is usually made of cotton and is often trimmed. All sorts of trimmings are suitable for swimsuits as long as they also meet all the necessary requirements of absolute colorfastness and general durability. Ruffles or permanent pleats are fine in matching or contrasting fabrics. A large variety of sturdy braids are also suitable trimmings. Appliqués can be used if the necessary machines are available in the factory. Colorfast embroideries are suitable as long as the stitching won't interfere with the stretch in the fabric. Buttons used on swimsuits must not rust, and therefore metal buttons or self-covered buttons with metal bases cannot be used.

In spite of all the special qualifications that swimsuits for children have to meet, they cannot be sold if they are too expensive. The designer must carefully stay within a rather rigid price structure. This limits the choice of fabrics not only to those that give high-quality performance, but also to those that are relatively inexpensive. Labor costs must be kept to a minimum without sacrificing a perfectly clean finish and construction that holds up under the most rugged wearing conditions. Trimmings, when used, must be sturdy but not costly.

The manufacturers who have become successful in the children's swimwear business have achieved this position by consistently turning out a reliable product at a saleable price. A certain trust is established between the manufacturer and the retailer, so that often the buyer will rely more than is usual on the advice of the manufacturer and the designer when making selections from the line. Needless to say, the designer in this position must be a real professional, one who not only has a good sense of design, but one who also, with experience, has learned to understand production and merchandising problems.

Sleepwear and Robes

There is perhaps no other area of children's wear design that offers as much opportunity for free expression as creating pajamas, nightgowns, and robes. For "at-home" wear, clothing can be imaginative and fanciful as long as it is also comfortable and washable. Little girls can look feminine and fragile in long ruffled gowns, or they may romp through the house in tomboy pajamas with a sportswear look. Robes, usually designed to match sleepwear, also can be either softly feminine or tailored. Current fashion finds its own expression in sleepwear and loungewear. For example, when the peasant look is popular, peasant prints and bright colors will appear in special fabrics for pajamas and nightgowns. These are then styled with their own peasant-inspired flair.

Designers prepare two major collections each year. The fall and winter collection includes sleepwear of brushed fabrics, and robes designed for warmth. For winter holiday selling, additional items especially designed for gift purchasing are usually added to the line. Accessories such as quilts that zip into sleeping bags, booties, curler caps, dolls, or pajama bags are designed to match coordinated groups of pajamas, nightgowns, and robes. The other major collection is for spring and summer selling. Fabrics are cool and airy. Pajamas may have bloomer panties or shorts instead of long legs. Nightgowns or pajama tops may be sleeveless or have short sleeves replacing the long sleeves that are required for winter garments. Robes for spring and summer either serve as cover-ups for skimpy pajamas or are designed in terrycloth for bath and beachwear.

SLEEPWEAR

The children's sleepwear market is roughly divided between two types of manufacturers: those who specialize in knitted garments and those who produce garments made of woven fabrics. There are a few large firms, however, that handle both woven and knitted goods.

The staple item for manufacturers of knit pajamas is the two-piece sleeper of heavy brushed cotton knit for winter and of lighter weight for spring. Winter sleepers have attached feet for warmth with a non-slip plastic sole covering for safety. Double sets of snaps attaching the trousers to the top at the waistline of Infants' and Toddler sizes provide extra room for growth. For the older child, the top of the sleeper is shaped like a pullover and the trouser waistlines are elasticized all around. For the spring and summer collections, the fabrics are light, airy, and absorbent knits of 100 percent cotton, or blends of cotton and polyester. The cut of the sleepers remains the same as for winter except that foot coverings are eliminated and sleeves are short.

These basic functional garments have been used for children for many years, but each season designers add that little something to make them appealing and just a little different. Appliqués and embroideries can be used for trimming. Color combinations can vary. New prints are used as well as solid colors. It is surprising what is done every season with an item that has not been changed in basic cut for more than two generations.

The following tables give the garment measurements for Infants', Children's, and Girls' knit pajamas as recommended by the United States Department of Commerce.

Table V—Infants' and Children's Two-piece Sleepers

SIZE	12 MO.	18 MO.	2	3	4
Top:					
Width of garment	10	11	11	12	12
Length	11	12	13	14	15
Sleeve length	9	10	11	12	13
Armhole length	5½	5½	6	6	6½
Neck opening	11	11	12	13	13
Waistband location	9	9½	10	10½	11
Pants:					
Waist circumference	20	21	22	22½	23
Front waistband length	10½	11	11½	12	12½
Total length:					
To heel of garment (with feet)	17	18½	20	22	24
Cuff (without feet)	16	17½	19	20½	22½
Front rise	8¾	9	9¼	9½	9¾
Back rise	9¾	10	10¼	10½	10¾
Width across seat	12½	13½	13½	14½	14½
Width of thigh	5½	6	6	6½	6½
Width of ankle	3¾	4	4	4¼	4½
Length of foot	6	6	6½	7	7½
Suit buttoned:					
Trunk	36½	38	39½	41	42½
Total length	26	28	30	32½	35

METHOD OF MEASURING

Top

Width of garment—Measured across the garment 1 inch below the bottom of the armhole.

Length—Measured from the point where the shoulder joins the collarette or neck opening to the bottom edge of the top.

Sleeve length—Measured in a straight line from the point under the arm where the sleeve is seamed to the garment to the lower outside edge of the sleeve, or sleeve cuff, if a cuff is usd.

Armhole length—Measured from the point where the sleeve is attached to the shoulder to the lowest point under the arm.

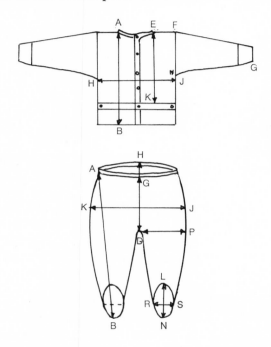

Neck opening—Measured by taking the circumference of the neck at the seam, from the center of the collarette button to the outside end of the buttonhole.

Location of waistband—Measured from the neck seam at the shoulder to the upper edge of the trouser when buttoned.

Pants

Waist circumference—Measured as twice the distance between the outside edges of the waistband, elastic relaxed and smooth.

Front waistband length—Measured from end to end of the front waistband.

Total length—Measured from the outside top edge of the waistband to the heel of the garment with the heel extended as the foot is folded back over the ankle of the garment.

Total length (cuff, without feet)—Measured from the outside top edge of the waistband to the bottom edge of the leg.

Front rise—Measured from the bottom of the crotch to the top edge of the waistband at center front.

Back rise—Measured from the bottom of the crotch to the top edge of the waistband at center back.

Width across seat—Measured across the back of the garment at a point halfway between the bottom of the crotch and the top edge of the waistband at center back.

Width of thigh—Measured across the leg at the bottom of the crotch.

Width of ankle—Measured across the leg where the foot is joined to the leg.

Length of foot—Measured from toe to heel of the bottom of the foot, with the foot laid out flat.

Suit Buttoned

Trunk—Measured as twice the distance from the point where the shoulder joins the collarette to the bottom of the crotch.

Table VI—Children's and Girls' Knit Pajamas

SIZE		2	4	6	7	8	10	12	14
Blouse:									
Width	(H-J)	11	12	13	14	14	15	16	17
Length	(A-B)	14½	16	17½	19	20	21½	23	24
Sleeve length	(N-G)	11	13	15	16½	17½	19	20	21
Armhole length	(F-N)	6	6½	7	7½	7½	8	8½	9
Neck opening:									
Ribbed knit		12	12½	13	13½	13½	14	14½	15
Stretched		20	20½	21	21½	21½	22	22½	23
Border rib length	(C-D)	3	3	3	3	3	3	3	3
Trousers:									
Waist circumference									
(All elastic web)	(A-C)	17	17¾	18½	19	19½	20	20¾	21½
Total length	(A-B)								
Rib bottom		20	23½	27½	31	32½	35½	37	38½
Hem bottom		19	22½	26½	30	31½	35½	36	37½
Front rise	(D-G)	9	10	10¾	11½	12¼	13	13¾	14½
Back rise	(D-H)	11	12	12¾	13	14¼	15	15¾	16½
Width across seat	(K-L)	13	14	15	16	17	18	19	20
Width of thigh	(D-N)	8	8½	9	9½	10	10½	11	11½
Leg-cuff length	(E-B)	4	4	4	4	4	4	4	4

METHOD OF MEASURING

Blouse

Width of garment—Measured across the garment 1 inch below the bottom of the armhole.

Length—Measured from the point where the shoulder joins the collarette to the bottom edge of the blouse.

Sleeve length—Measured in a straight line from the point under the arm where the sleeve is joined to the garment to the lower outside edge of the sleeve, or the sleeve cuff, if a cuff is used.

Armhole length—Measured from the point where the sleeve is attached to the shoulder to the lowest point under the arm.

Neck opening, flat—Measured by taking the circumference of the neck at the top edge with the fabric relaxed and smooth.

Neck opening, stretched—Measured by taking the circumference of the neck at the seam with the fabric stretched.

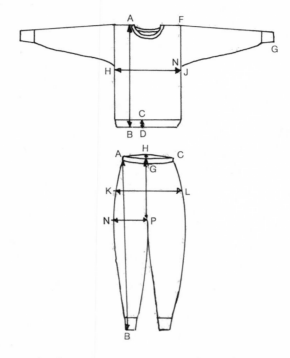

Border rib length—Measured from the middle of the seam attaching the rib to the edge of the blouse to the bottom edge of the border rib.

Trousers

Waist circumference—Measured as twice the distance between the outside edges of the waistband, elastic relaxed and smooth.

Total length—Measured from the outside top edge of the waistband to the bottom edge of the leg.

Front rise—Measured from the bottom of the crotch to the top edge of the waistband at center front.

Back rise—Measured from the bottom of the crotch to the top edge of the waistband at center back.

Width across seat—Measured across the back of the garment at a point halfway between the bottom of the crotch and the top edge of the waistband at center back.

Width of thigh—Measured across the leg at the bottom of the crotch.

Leg-cuff length—Measured from the middle of the seam attaching the cuff to the leg to the lower outside edge of the cuff.

Manufacturers in the other major area of sleepwear work primarily with woven fabrics: cotton flannels for fall and winter, and cotton and polyester batistes for spring and summer. Some firms also use tricot knits of nylon or acetate. These can be brushed for soft warmth for winter

wear. In general, nighties or pajamas of tricot combine excellent washability with a grown-up look. They are especially popular in 7-14 and Sub-teen sizes. Robes are designed in the same fabrics as sleepwear to form ensembles that can be merchandised together. Quilting is used to add extra body and warmth to winter robes. It is in this part of the industry that most of the exciting styling takes place. High fashion, fairy tales, sportswear, and the old and quaint all show their influence.

Since most manufacturers must produce good-looking, practical sleepwear at moderate prices, production has become extremely mechanized. Factories are equipped with the latest machinery, and in this area it is particularly important that the designer makes herself familiar with exactly what can be produced with the machinery at hand, and what could be done if additional investments were made in automated facilities. At present, almost all large manufacturers can do machine-smocking, quilting, tucking, appliqué, and small embroideries in their own plants.

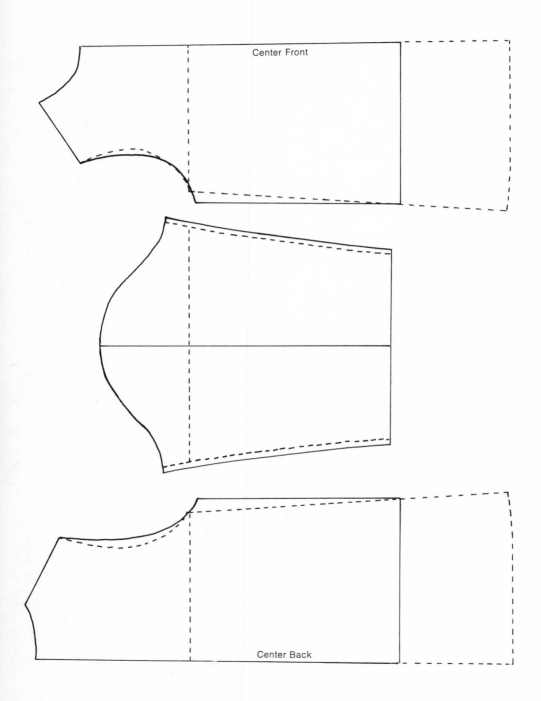

Special Problems

Nightgowns and pajamas must be cut so that they fit easily and comfortably with plenty of room for movement. Elastic, if used, must be soft, and buttons should be flat, so that no discomfort can interfere with sleep.

To adjust the basic pattern for a pajama top or nightgown:

1. Drop the armhole ¼ inch.
2. Extend the side seam ½ inch.
3. Straighten out the armhole as illustrated.
4. Mark off the length of the pajama top on the foundation pattern. Center-back length for a standard pajama top size 4 is 15¼ inches; for size 10 it is 19½ inches.
5. Adjust the sleeve pattern by flattening the cap 1 inch (see Shirtwaist Sleeve, page 115). Add ¼ inch at the underarm seam as illustrated.

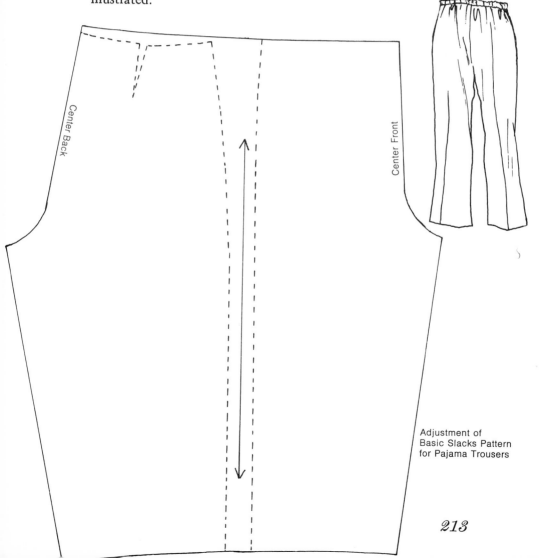

Center Back

Center Front

Adjustment of
Basic Slacks Pattern
for Pajama Trousers

213

To adjust the basic slacks patterns for pajama trousers:
1. Check crotch level. There should be a minimum of 1¼ inch ease.
2. Add ½ inch to the width at each side seam of both front and back (a total addition of 2 inches to the hip circumference).
3. Align front and back so that the lower sections of the side seam meet. The waistline is elasticized. Therefore the side seams and darts are eliminated.

To adjust the basic pattern for a robe:
Follom directions for the "Jacket" pattern adjustment (see page 198).

Underwear

Designing little girls' underwear can be very pleasant for a designer. This is especially true if she likes ruffles and lace and has a delicate touch. There are two kinds of children's underwear: the strictly functional white cotton-knit vest or shirt with panties, and the feminine, often delicately trimmed, slips and panties designed for gift-giving and impulse-buying. Both types may be made by the same manufacturer, but, more often, the basic shirts and panties are produced by the people who make cotton-knit underwear for both boys and girls in all size ranges, while the more highly designed type of girls' lingerie is made by the manufacturers who also produce sleepwear and loungewear. In most cases, different designers work for each of the various divisions within a firm, and separate factories are maintained for each specialty.

Basic vests and panties for girls are usually made from 1 x 1 ribbed or flat-knit cotton. The fabric is highly absorbent and comfortable in all sorts of climates. To aid in shape retention, special finishes are added or polyester is blended with the cotton. White is the basic color and is very practical for washing. But here lies a challenge for the designer. Perhaps the time is right for some color and excitement in this area. In any case, for the designers who want to try their hand at it, the following tables give the garment measurements for Girls' vests and panties as recommended by the United States Department of Commerce.

Table VII—Girls' Vests

SIZE		2	4	6	7	8	10	12	14
Width of garment	(C-D)	7½	8¼	9	9½	10	10½	11¼	12
Total length	(A-B)	16	18	20	21½	23*	24½	26	27½
Armhole length	(E-F)	6½	7	8	8	8½	9	9½	10
Neck opening		22	23½	25	26	27	28	29	30

METHOD OF MEASURING

Width of garment—measured across the garment 1 inch below the bottom of the armholes.

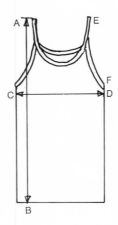

Total length—Measured from the top edge of the shoulder strap to the bottom edge of the vest.

Armhole length—Measured from the top point of the armhole at the shoulder along the outer edge of the armhole to the lowest point under the arm (half the length of the armhole band).

Neck opening—Measured by taking the circumference of the neck at the top edge with the fabric relaxed and smooth.

Table VIII—Girls' Panties

SIZE		2	4	6	7	8	10	12	14
Waist (circumference)									
elastic around	(A-C)	16	16¾	17½	17½	18¼	19	19¾	20½
Side length	(A-B)	6½	7¼	8	8½	9	9½	10	10½
Front rise	(D-G)	8¾	9¾	10½	11¼	12	12½	13	13½
Back rise	(D-H)	9¾	10¾	11½	12¼	13	13½	14	14½
Width across seat:	(K-L)								
ribbed (1 x 1)		10½	11¼	12	12¾	13½	14½	15½	16½
flat knit		11½	12¼	13	13¾	14½	15½	16½	17½
Leg opening									
ribbed-cuff style		9	10	11	12	13	14	15	16
Width across crotch	(F-J)	3½	3¾	4	4¼	4½	4¾	5	5

METHOD OF MEASURING

Waist (circumference)—Measured as twice the distance between the outside legs of the waistband, elastic relaxed and smooth.

Side length—Measured from the top outside edge of the waistband to the bottom edge of the leg opening at the side.

Front rise—Measured from the bottom of the crotch to the top edge of the waistband at center front.

Back rise—Measured from the bottom of the crotch to the top edge of the waistband at center back.

Width across seat—Measured across the back of the garment at the widest part.

Leg opening—Circumference, measured at the bottom edge.

Width across crotch—Measured between the outside edges at the bottom of the crotch.

A more feminine version of Girls' panties is made by the lingerie manufacturers who make slips. In addition to cotton knits, nylon or rayon tricot is used. These panties may be trimmed with lace, embroidery, or appliqué and are often bought as gifts.

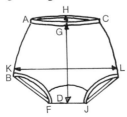

When slips aren't bought as gifts, they are usually bought to go with a particular dress or skirt. Therefore they must be designed to harmonize with the current fashion silhouette for girls. When full skirts are in fashion, crisp, ruffled slips or petticoats will make them stand out and look even fuller. When straight shifts are in, the soft nylon slip will underline the dress without adding any unnecessary bulk. A gentle A-line skirt needs a gentle A-line slip with perhaps just a ruffle at the lower edge to make the hem stand out.

Slips for girls may be full-length slips or half-slips. For toddlers and pre-school children the half-slip tends to slide down, so full slips are recommended. Schoolgirls and sub-teens like the half-slip or petticoat. To them it represents a more grown-up look, especially when the vest has given way to a "training bra."

All slips are designed with some sort of trimming. A little narrow Val lace to finish the neckline and the armholes may be all that is necessary for a toddler slip. To keep the outer edges of slips as light and delicate as possible, narrow laces applied with a zigzag stitch are used instead of hems or bindings. Delicate embroideries and appliquéed lace are also widely used as trimming. Ribbons laced through eyelet beading often add a touch of color, and for variety, there are stitching and tucking. It is important to remember that trimming on underwear should always be flat so that there won't be any unwanted bulky areas under the dress. All ribbon bows are pressed flat. Ruffles are only used on slips when they are deliberately placed to add width to the skirt of the outer garment. Pleated flounces are sometimes used when extra fabric is desired for movement, but the silhouette must be kept straight and smooth.

Fabrics for slips should be soft and comfortable, as well as washable with no need for ironing. Cotton and polyester batiste is used for all size ranges. For older girls, the grown-up look of nylon tricot is popular. When crisper fabrics are needed, woven nylon or nylon net may be used for ruffles. With these crisp fabrics care must be taken so that they do not rub or irritate the child's skin.

Slips and half-slips or petticoats can be cut in any way that dresses and skirts are cut. Princess seaming is often used. It permits an infinite variety of shapes, since as much or as little flare can be added as desired. Waistlines can be placed at any level: raised, normal, or lowered, depending on the silhouette that is wanted. For Infants' and Toddlers' sizes, slips are cut with built-up shoulder straps, because narrow straps tend to slip down from small shoulders. For 3-6x and 7-14 sizes, shoulder straps can be adjustable ribbons, the same as are used in adult lingerie. Slips may be worn over a vest, but in many cases are worn just with panties for a pretty lingerie look. They should be cut to softly hug the upper part of the body so that there is no unnecessary bulk under dresses or blouses. Many slips are designed with an elasticized panel at the side seam for flexible fit (see illustration).

A slip should fit fairly close to the body and should be cut low enough at the underarm so that it won't show when the child wears a sleeveless dress. To adjust the basic shift pattern for a slip:

1. Drop the armhole ¼ inch.
2. Reduce width at the side seam and armhole ½ inch.
3. Draw in the built-up shoulder straps as illustrated.

4. When ribbon straps are used, they must be placed no farther apart than the center of the shoulder; otherwise they tend to slip off the shoulders of the child.

5. Shorten basic pattern at least 1 inch.

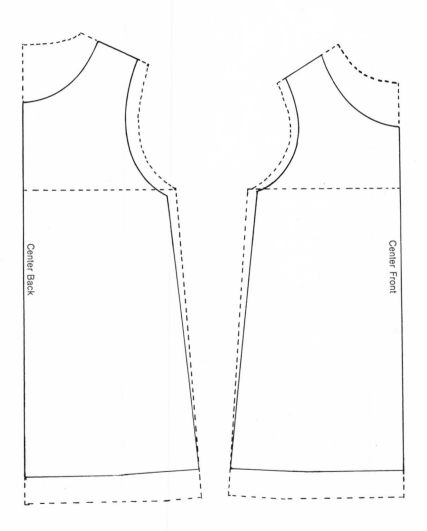

Outerwear

Designers of children's outerwear create dress coats, sport coats, and waterproof raincoats. They design jackets of various lengths and weights, as well as snowsuits and ski suits.

With the development of the new man-made fiber fabrics, outdoor clothing for children has undergone some revolutionary changes. Acrylic pile linings and polyester fiberfill insulation have made outerwear of virtually weightless fabrics entirely practical. Heavy, cumbersome garments have been replaced by washable, comfortably warm, protective clothing. Whereas the warm wool overcoat was a necessity for daily winter wear a generation ago, it is now used only for special occasions. Many children never own one. They stay dry and comfortable in all sorts of weather with lightweight but warmly insulated coats or jackets.

Outerwear manufacturers fall into two general categories. The traditional coat manufacturers make coats for either boys or girls that are mostly cut from wool fabrics. Coats of acrylic pile or other novelty fabrics are included in most collections, but, by and large, these manufacturers make conventional coats, warmly interlined for winter and in lighter weights for spring. Other outerwear manufacturers, those that may have originally started out as snowsuit producers, are now making a comprehensive line for both boys and girls. These manufacturers may make garments in all size ranges: for babies, buntings and pram bags; for toddlers and pre-school youngsters, snowsuits, raincoats, and jackets; and for the older child, there are duffle coats, trench coats, and other kinds of sportcoats and raincoats in addition to ski suits and all sorts of odd jackets.

Outerwear manufacturers present two lines each year. The Winter line must be ready in March and is shown until August. The Spring line opens in September and is shown until February. During such a long selling season it must be expected that new numbers will be added here and there to meet immediate selling needs of the retailer. On the other hand, mail-order catalogues are planned so far in advance that the designer may be called upon to design special numbers for the catalogues far in advance of the regular collection.

Sample sizes for outerwear differ somewhat from the other areas of children's apparel. For the Toddler size range, 2T-4T, sample size is 4T. If the sample looks well in a size 4, the manufacturer may run the number from size 2 to 6x, spanning two size ranges. This is particularly practical for snowsuits and raincoats since styling for the younger and older pre-school child doesn't vary much in these areas. Samples of styles that are to be run only in the 3-6x size range are usually made in size 5. Sample size for 7-14 is size 10.

The designer working for a traditional coat house often only submits sketches. She selects fabrics and trimmings, but an expert patternmaker takes over to cut the first sample, and skilled tailors take care of the construction. For the comprehensive outerwear house, on the other hand, the designer often cuts the first sample and works with a sample-maker as in other children's wear areas. To save time, occasionally only the fronts of coats and jackets may be made in the sample room. This is especially true for snowsuits and ski suits. The jackets are completed and matching pants are added in the factory. Aside from enabling the sample room to turn out many more samples, this practice results in samples that are finished exactly like stock garments, an effect that is difficult to achieve when special machinery is not available in the sample room.

The tailored dress coat requires a very special kind of styling. In a way, this is the area of children's wear that is closest to designing for adults. To begin with, there are the classics. These are the basic, practical coats that develop gradually and recur periodically whenever they seem right in adult fashion. Among these styles are polo or boy coats, trench coats, and princess coats. The princess coat for children has been a perennial favorite. Shaped at the waist and with a moderately flared skirt, it is a flattering silhouette for most little girls. Many stores have traditionally imported these coats from England, where fine tailoring is a specialty. Made from good, durable tweeds and plaid wools, these coats are made

to last, and have been handed down from child to child in many families. Besides the classics, every coat line must also include many more highly styled models. Winter coats are sometimes trimmed with fur. Leather and velveteen are also used as trimming. Many dress coats for children have hats designed to match. For the little sizes, matching leggings may be sold with the coat. The spring coat, often referred to in the trade as the "Easter Coat," is usually designed in pastels or light, bright colors. Many children's dress houses compete with the coat manufacturers for the spring-coat business by designing ensembles of matching coats and dresses. Dress manufacturers, however, do not have the skilled labor available to produce a tailored coat, and the ensemble coat is usually designed without the interlinings and tailoring details of the conventional coat.

All coats must be designed with collars of some sort. Either a built-up neckline or a collar is needed to cover the neckline of dresses or blouses.

When the necklines of these garments are exposed, they should match the coat, or the general effect is spoiled. Since most children are not likely to wear coordinated coats and dresses, it is best to always include a collar and have the coat button right up to the neckline. Another feature essential in designing coats is pockets. Most children don't carry handbags, and pockets are needed for handkerchiefs, occasional change, and other little necessities. Therefore pockets should not only be worked into every coat, but they should also be big enough to hold a few things.

The basic pattern must be enlarged for a coat foundation pattern. Coats should fit easily over normal indoor clothing, and patterns must be large enough to compensate for the bulk of heavy coating fabric, lining, and interlining. The measurements, below, may be varied according to the type of fabric used and the bulk of the lining or interlining. For example, the bulk of a quilted lining is usually greater than the bulk of acrylic pile, and both are bulkier than a conventional wool interlining.

To cut a coat, it is best to begin with the shift sloper. For the average adjustment of the shift pattern for a coat:

1. Lower the neckline ⅛ inch all around.
2. Raise the shoulder ¼ inch at the armhole.
3. Extend the shoulder ¾ inch at the armhole.
4. Lower the armhole 1 inch.
5. Extend the side seam 1 inch.
6. Slash the sleeve as illustrated. Spread ¼ inch at the center vertical slash, ⅜ inch at the other vertical slashes, and ½ inch at the horizontal slashes.

When designing outerwear for the manufacturer who produces a comprehensive line, the designer must be especially aware of the possibilities inherent in the new fabrics and the needs of active children. The coats made by these manufacturers are often called sport coats and are designed for play and general daily wear. Included are usually duffle coats, peacoats, trench coats, and other kinds of raincoats. Fabrics may be closely woven cotton and polyester blends, or nylon. Other fabrics may be coated with polyurethane film to provide a waterproof finish. Acrylic-pile fabrics may be used as linings or as the outer shell in coats that resemble fur of every species. The general styling of these coats is usually inspired by the current fashion in adult sportswear. The most important points for the designer to consider are: Is it rugged? Is it comfortable? Does it have the look of today?

Snowsuits and ski suits are the other major items in outerwear for children. For the small child, the dress coat is a luxury, and raincoats are hardly necessary. Most toddlers manage very well with only a snowsuit in their winter wardrobes. Snowsuits for boys and girls must be washable and water repellent. Colors range from pastel to navy, with clear, bright hues in between. Quilted nylon or plain nylon shells with acrylic-pile linings are most popular. Acrylic-pile jackets are often teamed

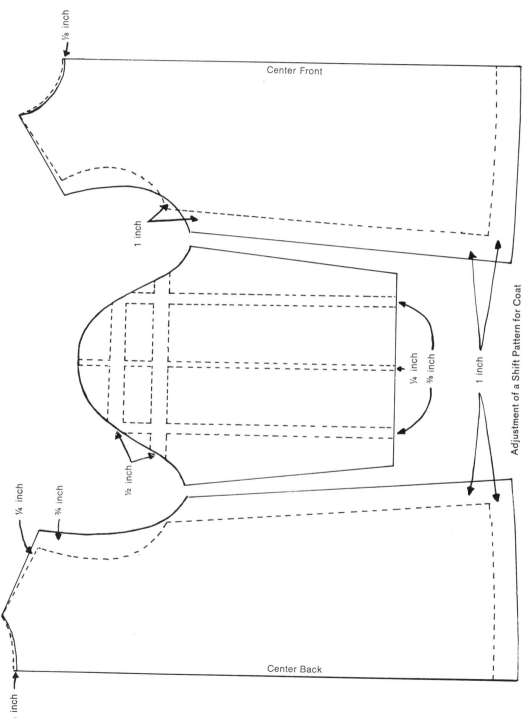

⅛ inch

Center Front

1 inch

¼ inch

⅜ inch

1 inch

½ inch

¼ inch

¾ inch

⅛ inch

Center Back

⅛ inch

Adjustment of a Shift Pattern for Coat

with harmonizing nylon snowpants. Contrasting colors, embroidery, stitching, or braid are used as trimmings. Although most snowsuits consist of a jacket and pants, one-piece snowsuits are preferred by some mothers. They find it easier and faster to dress small children when there is just one garment to handle. Generally, snowsuits have zipper closings, and these may also be handled in a decorative manner. Many snowsuits are designed with hoods attached to the jacket. Hoods should have a drawstring or tab that fastens securely under the chin. Nothing is as annoying as a hood that won't stay in place. When there is no hood attached to

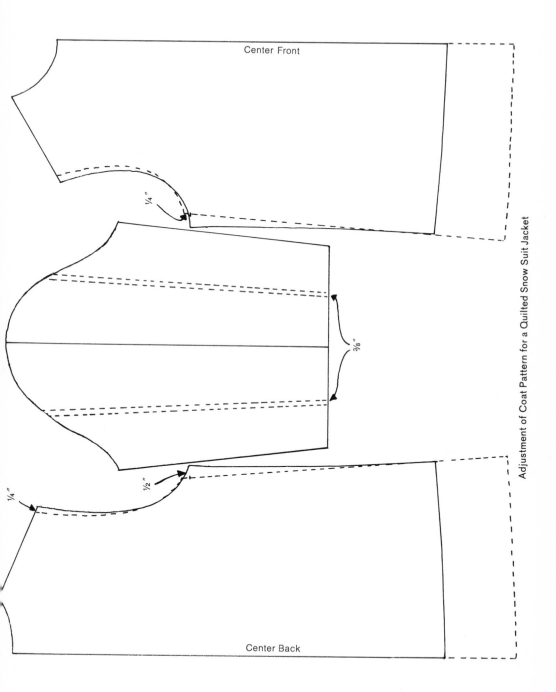

Center Front

¼"

⅜"

Adjustment of Coat Pattern for a Quilted Snow Suit Jacket

½"

¼"

Center Back

the jacket, the snowsuit is usually sold with a matching hat. Girls' hats tie securely under the chin, and boys' caps are designed with a visor and ear flaps as well as a chin strap that is closed with snaps.

For the 7-14 group, the snowsuit has evolved into the ski parka that is sold with separate ski pants. Parkas are often worn with all sorts of school and play clothes and in many cases never see a ski slope. The styling, however, is patterned strictly on adult ski wear. Quilted nylon, both printed and plain, acrylic pile, and vinyls that resemble leather are all used. Ski pants are usually cut in water-repellent stretch nylon for this age group and are patterned after their adult counterparts.

For snowsuits and ski suits certain design features are essential. Openings should all be windproof and close snugly. Necklines have attached hoods or well-fitted collars. Sometimes turtleneck dickeys and scarfs are included in the design. Wrist openings have rib-knit cuffs or are equipped with an inside cuff for a windproof finish. Some parkas have sleeves that are elasticized at the wrist. Ski pants have straps that fit under the instep or ribbing at the ankle, so that the pants stay securely inside the boots. For Toddler and 3-6x sizes, ski pants must be suspended from the shoulders. Pants are often built up, but when simple suspenders are used, the waistline is elasticized.

To cut a snowsuit jacket or ski parka, the same basic adjustment as for the coat pattern may be used (see page 224). For a quilted jacket additional ease must be added:

1. Extend the shoulder an additional ¼ inch.
2. Lower the armhole an additional ¼ inch.
3. Extend the side seam an additional ½ inch.
4. For a size 4, mark length of jacket 18 inches at center back.
5. Shape side seam very slightly as illustrated.
6. Slash the coat sleeve pattern vertically, as illustrated, and spread ¼ inch on each side.

Boys' Wear

INFANTS

During the first year of a child's life, there is very little difference between boys' and girls' clothing. Shirts, nighties, diapers, and plastic pants are styled identically for both sexes. At this stage, from booties to buntings, often the only difference between boys' and girls' wear is in the color, pink for girls and blue for boys. Although the basic cut of the garment is usually the same, there is sometimes a difference in the use of trimmings. Ruffles and bows are reserved for girls, while more tailored touches are used for boys' clothing. Collars are squared off rather than rounded for boy's wear. Sleeves are tailored and never puffed. Trimmings are flat and neat. Embroidery and appliqués can be cute and whimsical but never flowery.

TODDLER SIZES

When a boy reaches the toddler stage, his clothing has developed some more distinct features. Most obviously, on dress-up occasions boys now wear pants and most girls wear skirts. Although girls and women also wear slacks as well as skirts, boys and men traditionally wear trousers for all occasions. There are other distinctions. The generally tailored look of boys' wear requires fabrics with more body and a firmer weave. The piece-goods houses take their cue and develop special fabrics for the boys' wear market. To complete their wardrobes, boys need shirts in woven as well as knitted fabrics. They need jackets designed in various weights for winter, transitional, and summer weather.

In the Toddler sizes, jackets are often designed to match pants. For spring and fall, these outfits are cut in corduroy or cotton twill with flannel linings for lightweight warmth. Winter jackets are lined with acrylic pile or quilted linings for extra warmth. For special occasions, little boys may wear shorts and shirt outfits in dressy fabrics; for example, velveteen shorts with a linen shirt, or matching shorts and shirt out of fine cotton broadcloth in pastel colors. One-piece jumpsuits are also becoming increasingly popular for little boys.

Colors are generally light and bright for toddler clothing. Embroideries and appliqués are used freely for trimmings. Edgings, when used for boys, are somewhat restrained, and it is better not to get any frilly effects. Contrasting cording, piping, or stitching usually work well to underline and emphasize any design features.

Firms manufacturing Toddler sizes often make both boys' and girls' wear. Sometimes matching outfits are sold for brother and sister. Jumpers for girls and overalls for boys are cut out of the same fabric and teamed with matching shirts and blouses. Dresses and suits designed to harmonize lend themselves to attractive displays and advertising.

CHILDREN'S SIZES

For the 3-7 size range, much of the toddler cuteness is replaced by a more tailored look. The pre-school boy is very active and needs rugged clothing for indoor and outdoor play. Most manufacturers producing boys' clothing in this size range are specialists in boys' wear. Trimmings and embroideries are almost completely eliminated. Overalls suspended from the shoulders or slacks with elasticized waistbands are paired with knitted shirts for daily wear. Corduroy, denim, or sturdy weaves of polyester and cotton are used for the trousers. Combined with a knitted shirt, this is a comfortable and protective outfit for active play. If well constructed, this sort of clothing is easily laundered and wears well. For spring and fall, jackets and sweaters are needed. Outerwear manufacturers provide the snowsuits, heavy jackets, or duffle coats needed for winter. Raincoats are also a necessary item, and these are made of plastic-coated cotton or other waterproof material. The Eton suit with its collarless jacket and short pants is popular for parties and other special occasions. By the time a boy is six or seven years old, however, he will prefer a sport jacket or blazer with long trousers, just like his older brother.

We shall limit our discussion here to boys' wear problems in the 2-4 and 3-7 size ranges. Creating boys' wear in the 7-20 range requires the same methods of tailoring and design as men's wear and is beyond the scope of this volume.

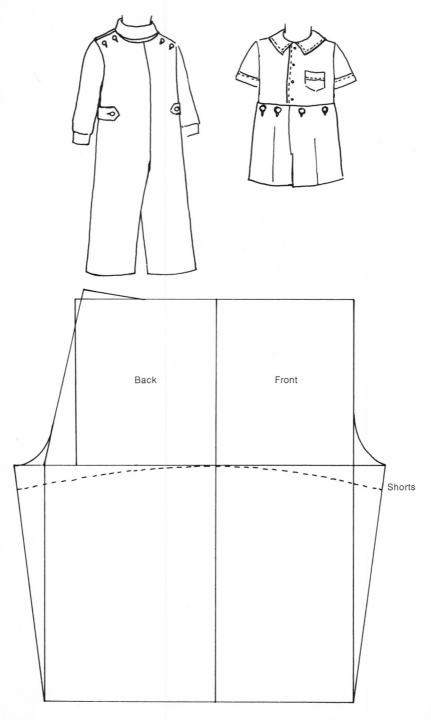

Back

Front

Shorts

Special Problems

Toddler Trousers

Trousers for toddler boys are constructed very simply. Sample size is usually size 2. There is no front placket opening, and since the child has no waist development, trousers are usually attached to the shirt or suspended from the shoulders.

To cut toddler trousers:

1. Draft slacks (see page 161). Allow 1 inch ease in the crotch and ¾ inch ease at the hip. There will be no need for darts or shaping at the waistline. When the legs are not tapered, the side seam may be eliminated as in infants' wear.
2. For shorts, measure to the crotch level at the side seam and 1 inch down at the inseam. Connect guide markings as illustrated.

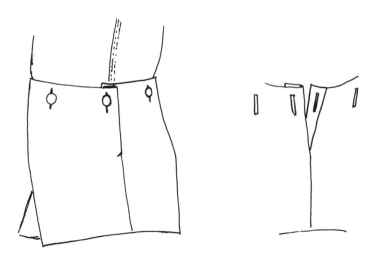

When shorts button to the shirt, allow a deep hem or facing at the waistline to provide backing for buttonholes. A placket is constructed at the side seam, and overlapping buttonholes from front and back button to the shirt at the side seam.

To cut a jump suit or overalls:

1. Separate trouser pattern at the side seam.
2. Place the front and back waist slopers so that the waistline of the front sloper meets the waistline of the trousers at center front. Align back waist to front waist at the underarm.
3. Blend in side seam and center-back seam as illustrated. There will be a space in the waistline area at the side seam and center back. This is necessary for fit in a jumpsuit.
4. For built-up overalls, draw style lines on the basic jumpsuit pattern.

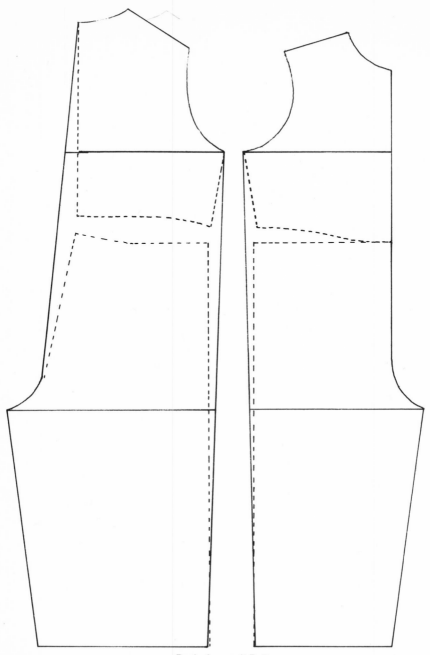

Basic Jumpsuit Pattern

The Boys' Dress Shirt

This is the shirt, cut from woven fabrics, that complements the Eton suit or may be worn with any kind of shorts or overalls. Sometimes dress shorts of velveteen, linen, or fine cotton are designed to button onto the shirt. The collar may be rolled or flat. Sleeves may be long or short, and the shirt closing may be plain or finished with a band. A patch pocket

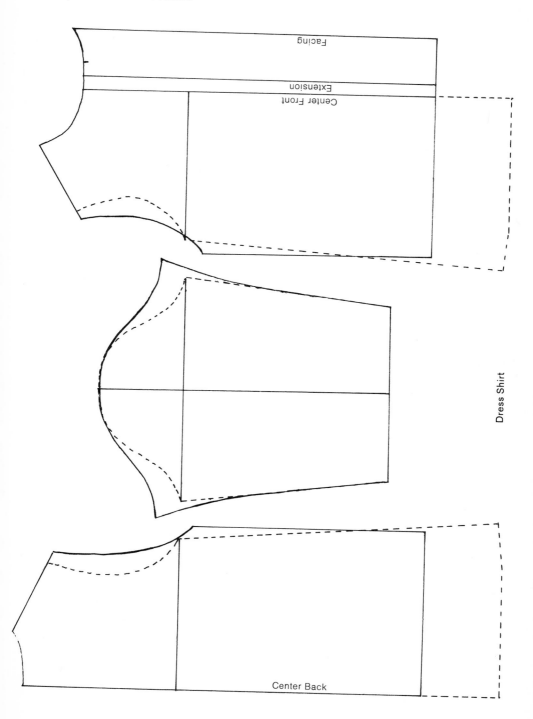

Facing

Extension

Center Front

Dress Shirt

Center Back

is sometimes applied to the left front of the shirt. Sleeve caps are flattened. The armhole is straightened out and somewhat enlarged to create a roomy, comfortable garment that can be easily sewn with double-needle construction.

To cut a boys' shirt it is best to use the shift sloper. For size 4:

1. Mark the length of the shirt at the center-back seam at 16½ inches.
2. Extend the shoulder ½ inch at the armhole; drop the armhole ½ inch at the underarm; add ½ inch to the width of the shirt at the side seam.
3. Add extension for buttons at the center front.
4. Plan band if desired.
5. Add facings at center front.
6. Flatten the cap of the sleeve sloper an additional 1 inch. Ease in the sleeve cap should not exceed ½ inch.

The following table gives the garment measurements for Boys' size sport and dress shirts as recommended by the United States Department of Commerce for sizes 4, 6, and 8. Measurements for size 2 were not available in this category and were extrapolated for sport shirts.

Table IX

		SPORTS SHIRT				DRESS SHIRT		
	SIZE	2	4	6	8	4	6	8
(N)	Neckline	11	11½	12	12½	11	11½	12
(C)	Chest	25	27	29	31	27	29	31
(L)	Length	15½	17	18½	20	19	21	22½
(A)	Armhole girth	11	12	13	14	12	13	14
(Y)	Yoke width	10¾	11½	12¼	13	11½	12¼	13
(S)	Sleeve length	17½	19	21½	23½	19	21½	23½

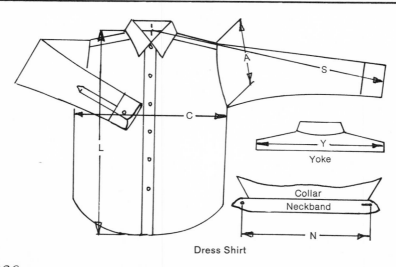

Dress Shirt

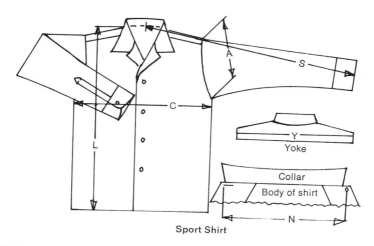

Sport Shirt

METHODS OF MEASURING

Neckline—Measured from the center of the button parallel to the neckline to the far end of the buttonhole.

Chest—Twice the distance across the buttoned-up shirt, measured to its outer limits, 1 inch below the bottom of the armhole.

Length—Measured from the highest point of the yoke to the bottom of the shirt when the front and back lengths are even at the bottom.

Armhole girth—Twice the distance across the sleeve at the armhole, measured in a straight line from the top to the bottom of the armhole.

Yoke width—Measured across the body of the yoke where it joins the body of the garment.

Sleeve length—Measured from the center of the yoke to the bottom of the cuff.

The Knit Polo or T-Shirt

Knit shirts are popular for everybody because they are comfortable and simple to care for. Even before the days of permanent press, cotton-knit shirts could be laundered and worn without the benefit of an iron. Most boys like these shirts for their free and easy fit and comfortable, soft texture.

To cut a size 4 knit shirt from a shift sloper:

1. Mark the length at the center back—15½ inches.
2. Reduce the width of the sloper at the underarm—¾ inch.
3. Drop the armhole ½ inch and straighten the armhole as illustrated.
4. Flatten the cap of the sleeve 1½ inches, and reduce the width of the sleeve so that there is no more than ½ inch ease in the

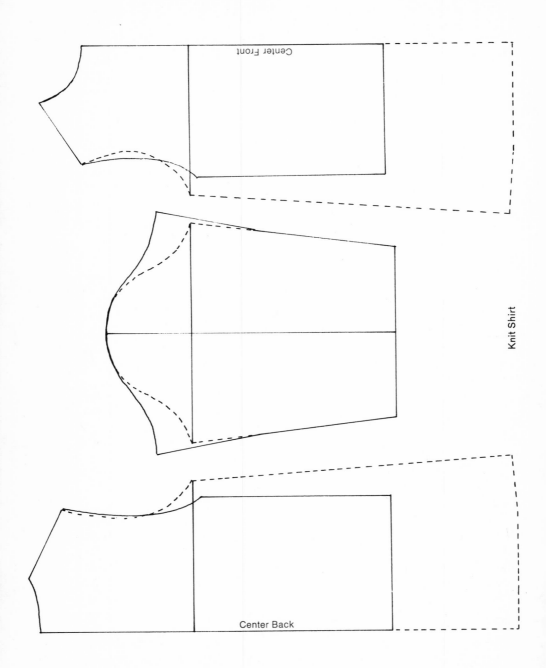

Center Front

Knit Shirt

Center Back

238

sleeve cap. Smooth out some of the shaping in the sleeve cap as illustrated.

The following table gives the garment measurements for Boys' size knit shirts as recommended by the United States Department of Commerce for sizes 2, 4, 6, and 8.

Table X

SIZE	2	4	6	8
Width of garment	10½	11½	12½	13¼
Total length	14½	16	17½	19
Sleeve length:				
Short, underarm	3½	4	4	4½
Long, underarm	10½	12½	14½	16
Armhole length	5	5½	6	6½
Collar length for polo shirt	11½	12	12½	13
Ribbed-knit neckline for T-shirt	12	12½	13	13½
Stretched	20	20½	21	21½

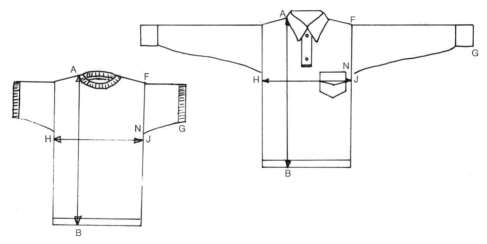

METHODS OF MEASURING

Width of Garment—Measured across the garment 1 inch below the bottom of the armholes. (H to J)

Total length—Measured from the point where the shoulder joins the collar to the bottom edge of the shirt. (A to B)

Sleeve length—Measured from the point under the arm where the sleeve is seamed to the garment to the lower edge of the sleeve, or of the sleeve cuff, if a cuff is used. (N to G)

Armhole length—Measured from the point where the sleeve is attached to the shoulder to the lowest point under the arm. (F to N)

Collar length—Measured from the center of the collar button around the neckband to the outside end of the buttonhole.

Ribbed-knit neckline—Measured by taking the circumference of the neck with the fabric relaxed and smooth.

Boys' Trousers with Front Placket

By the time a little boy is three or four years old, his trousers are cut, more or less, like mens' wear trousers. Typical features are the front placket opening and pockets. Legs may be straight, tapered, or flared according to the current style.

To cut boys' trousers in size 4 with a simplified front placket opening:

1. Use the basic slacks pattern (see page 161).

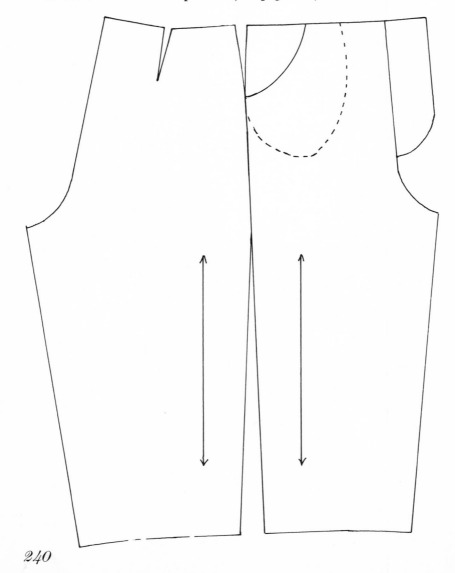

2. Plan pockets. Mark off pocket opening on the front pattern.
3. Indicate the shape of the inside pocket.
4. Add a placket extension, 1¾ inches wide and 6 inches long, at the center front. This will accommodate a 6-inch zipper.

To construct a simplified front placket opening on little boys' slacks:

1. Overedge the seam allowance of the placket extension.
2. Place zipper, face up, on left side front so that the right edge of the zipper tape is ¼ inch away from the extension. Stitch left zipper tape to the extension.

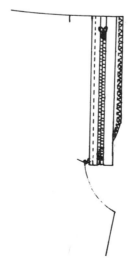

3. Enclose left zipper tape by folding the extension over the edge of the tape, forming a pleat. Topstitch into place.

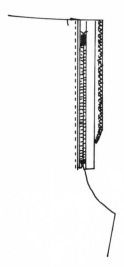

4. Place the right front over the left front so that center-front notches and waistline match. Crotch seam should also match. Stitch zipper to the right extension along the edge of the right zipper tape. Stitch crotch seam.

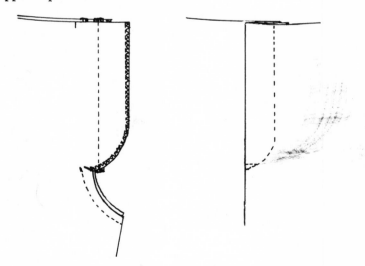

5. Turn to the right side. Straighten out fold of placket on the right extension, and stitch the placket about 1¼ inches from the center front, curving the lower end. Tack lower end of the placket at the center front, and topstitch the entire front crotch seam.

The following table gives garment measurements for Boys' size trousers as recommended by the United States Department of Commerce for sizes 4, 5, 6, and 7.

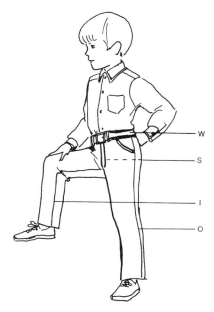

Table XI

SIZE		4	5	6	7
Waist	(W)	22½	22½	23	23½
Seat	(S)	28½	29½	30½	31½
Front rise [1]	(FR)	9¼	9½	9¾	10
Back rise [1]	(BR)	12½	12¾	13	13¼
Outseam finished [2]	(O)	23	25¼	27	28¾
Inseam finished	(I)	15	17	18½	20

[1] Rise measurements are based on trousers extending ¾ inch above waistline of boy.
[2] Difference in inches between outseam and inseam is true rise or crotch measurement.

METHODS OF MEASURING

Waist—Twice the distance across the waist of the trousers with the waistband smooth and flat. (If elastic waistbands are used, then the waist should be measured reasonably taut.)

Seat—About 2 inches above the crotch, measure the distance straight across the trousers, with the back seat fully pulled out.

Front rise—Measured from the crotch up along the edge of the fly to the top of the waistband.

Back rise—Measured from the crotch up the back seam of the trousers to the top of the waistband.

Outseam—Measured from the top of the waistband along side seam to the bottom of the cuff.

Inseam—With one leg thrown back over the upper part of the trousers, measure from the crotch seam to the bottom edge of the cuff.

Appendix

THE following tables of size designations and body measurements are taken from the *Commercial Standard on Body Measurements* developed by the United States Department of Commerce at the request of The Mail Order Association of America. The *Commercial Standards on Body Measurements for Infants, Babies, Toddlers, Children and Subteens* have been in effect for some time and are generally accepted and approved by the industry. The *Standard Body Measurements for the Sizing of Girls' Apparel* is relatively new and a revision of the older product standard in this area.

The new body measurements for school-age girls take into account that the body build of some children is slimmer than average, and that other children are chubbier than average. Therefore there are three classifications for this age group:

(a) "Slims"—identified by size number plus the designation "S."
(b) "Regulars"—identified by size number plus the designation "R."
(c) "Chubbies"—identified by size number plus the designation "½."
The height of girls in all classifications is the same for each size. The differences in the three classifications appear in the girth (and weight) measurements.

All the measurements in the following tables represent "Body Measurements" taken over light underwear, such as a vest and panties. To convert them to "Nude" measurements, the following amounts may be subtracted:

Chest—¾″ for all sizes
Waist—½″ for all sizes
Hip—¾″ for all sizes
Vertical trunk girth—1″ for all sizes
Total crotch length—½″ for all sizes
These "Body Measurements" serve as a guide for the manufacture of Model Forms and for the sizing and grading of garment patterns. "Garment Measurements" are arrived at after the necessary ease has been added. For example:

Size 4 Chest Body Measurement—23″
Size 4 Chest Dress Measurement—25″
Size 4 Chest Coat Measurement—29″

Stretchable knitted garments may measure less than body girth. For example, the chest measurement of a size 4 rib-knit polo shirt equals 21 inches.

Garment lengths depend on the proportions desired by the designer. Dress lengths vary depending on the effect desired. Coats should cover dresses completely, and therefore should be 1 to 2 inches longer than dresses. It is highly desirable that designers work with a full-length model form or use live models to establish the correct length of each garment.

DEFINITIONS OF BODY LANDMARKS

Definitions of the more important body landmarks shown in figure 1 are as follows:

a. Crown—Top of head, Figure 1.

b. Cervicale—The prominent point on the seventh or lowest cervicale vertebra at the back of the neck, Figure 1, which becomes more prominent when the head is bent forward. (Cervicale height measurements are taken, however, only when the head is in an erect position.)

c. Waist—The lower edge of the lower floating rib, located at the side of the body in a line directly below the center of the armpit.

d. Hip—The outer bony prominence of the upper end of the thigh bone (the femur).

e. Knee—The inner bony prominence of the upper end of the tibia, the larger of the two long bones of the leg extending from knee to ankle.

f. Ankle—The inner bony prominence of the lower end of the tibia, the larger of the two long bones of the leg extending from knee to ankle.

Figure 1

Appendix

METHODS OF MEASURING[1]

Vertical

Stature—Measure from crown to soles of feet.

Cervicale height—Measure from cervicale to soles of feet.

Waist height—Measure from waist to soles of feet. This waist height establishes the waist level around the body.

Hip height—Measure from hip to soles of feet.

Knee height—Measure from knee to soles of feet.

Ankle height—Measure from ankle to soles of feet.

Girth measurements.[2]

Chest—Measure horizontally close up under arms. The measurement should include the lower portion of the shoulder blades, Figure 2.

Waist—Measure horizontally at waist height, Figure 2.

Hip—Measure horizontally at hip height, Figure 2.

Vertical trunk—Measure from a point on the shoulder, midway between the neck and the normal armhole line, through the crotch, G through F to G, Figure 3. The measurement should be taken without constriction at the crotch.

Thigh—Measure horizontally around the upper part of the leg, close up to the crotch, H through F to H, Figure 3.

Figure 2

Figure 3

[1] Body measurements are recorded to the nearest ⅛ inch. More complete information regarding the methods of measuring the body may be obtained from *Miscellaneous Publication No. 336* of the U.S. Department of Agriculture.

[2] Girth measurements in this Standard include an allowance for clothing. Where measurements are taken over indoor clothing, it is assumed that customary undergarments are worn beneath.

Neck base—Measure around the neck touching the cervicale at the back and the upper borders of the collarbone at the front, following the curve that would be made by a fine-linked chain passing over these landmarks, B through J to B, figures 4 and 5.

Armscye—Measure from a point at the armhole edge of the shoulder, midway between the acromion and the highest prominence at the outer end of the collarbone, through the underarm midpoint, K around the arm to K, Figures 4 and 5.

Upper arm—Measure from a point midway between the outer edge of the shoulder and the elbow, around the arm at U level, Figure 3.

Figure 4

Figure 5

Width and Length Measurements

Cross-back width—Measure across the back from armscye to armscye, halfway between the cervicale and the bottom of the armscye, L to L¹, Figure 5.

Shoulder length—Measure from most lateral point of neck-girth measurement at shoulder to the armscye-girth point on the shoulder. S, Figure 5.

Total crotch length—Measure from waist level at the front, through the crotch, to the waist level at the back, C through crotch to C¹, Figure 6. (For waist level, see Figure 1, Waist height.)

Shoulder and arm length—Measure from the intersection of the neck and shoulder lines along the outside (posterior) surface of the arm, with the elbow flexed, to the prominent wristbone at the back of the hand, O to M, Figure 7.

Scye depth—Measure along the spine from the cervicale to a point level with the mid-underarm point, B to SD, Figure 5.

Total posterior arm length—Measure from the outer edge of shoulder over flexed elbow to wrist, N to M, figure 7.

Figure 6

Figure 7

Table I—Infants' and Babies' * Body Measurements
(Composite for boys' and girls' measurements)

MEASUREMENT	SIZE					
	3 MO.	6 MO.	12 MO.	18 MO.	24 MO.	36 MO.
Stature—inches	24	26½	29	31½	34	36½
Weight—pounds (approx.)	13	18	22	26	29	32
GIRTH MEASUREMENTS						
Chest	17	18	19	20	21	22
Vertical trunk	27	29	31	32½	34½	36½
LENGTH MEASUREMENT						
Shoulder and arm length	9	10¼	11½	12½	13¾	15
**VERTICAL MEASUREMENTS ** **						
Head and neck length	5¾	6	6⅛	6⅜	6⅝	6¾
Cervicale height	18¼	20½	22⅞	25⅛	27⅜	29¾
Cervicale to knee	13	14½	16⅛	17½	18¾	20⅜
Cervicale to waist, including curve of spine	6⅛	6⅞	7½	8	8⅜	8¾
Waist height	12⅛	13⅝	15½	17⅜	19¼	21⅛
Waist to knee	6⅞	7¾	8¾	9⅝	10⅝	11⅝
Waist to hip	2⅝	2⅞	3⅛	3½	3⅞	4¼
Crotch height	7¾	9⅛	10½	11⅞	13¼	14⅝
Knee height	5¼	6	6¾	7⅝	8½	9⅜

* The principal difference between the classifications "Infants" and "Babies" is a merchandising difference. Infants' garments are to be made in one size only, babies' in more than one (see Tables III, page 251 and IV, page 251).

** Since even gradations in vertical body measurements between sizes serves to make this standard more useful in grading garment patterns or specifications, minor adjustments (⅛ inch) have been made in a few instances to achieve this purpose.

Table II—Grade Chart for Babies' and Infants' Sizes

	GRADE BETWEEN 3 MO.-6 MO.	GRADE BETWEEN 6 MO.-12 MO.	GRADE BETWEEN 12 MO.-18 MO.	GRADE BETWEEN 18 MO.-24 MO.	GRADE BETWEEN 24 MO.-36 MO
GIRTH MEASUREMENTS (inches)					
Chest	1	1	1	1	1
Vertical trunk	2	2	1½	2	2
LENGTH MEASUREMENT (inches)					
Shoulder and arm length	1¼	1¼	1	1¼	1¼
VERTICAL MEASUREMENTS (inches)					
Head and neck length	¼	⅛	¼	¼	⅛
Cervicale height	2¼	2⅜	2¼	2¼	2⅜
Cervicale to knee	1½	1⅝	1⅜	1¼	1⅝
Cervicale to waist, including curve of spine	¾	⅝	½	⅜	⅜
Waist height	1½	1⅞	1⅞	1⅞	1⅞
Waist to knee	⅞	1	⅞	1	1
Waist to hip	¼	¼	⅜	⅜	⅜
Crotch height	1⅜	1⅜	1⅜	1⅜	1⅜
Knee height	¾	¾	⅞	⅞	⅞

Appendix

Table III—Standard Size Range for Certain Infants' Garments

	SIZE		
GARMENT	3 MO.	6 MO.	12 MO.
Gowns	Normally made in		
Layettes	only one of the		
Sweaters	above sizes.		
Wrappers			

Table IV—Standard Size Range for Certain Babies' * Garments

	SIZE**					
GARMENT	3 MO.	6 MO.	12 MO.	18 MO.	24 MO.	36 MO.
	UNDERWEAR					
Pants, rubber	X	X	X	X		
Pants, training			X	X	X	X
Shirts	X	X	X	X	X	
	OUTERWEAR					
Coats		X	X	X		
Creepers		X	X	X		
Dresses		X	X	X		
Sunsuits		X	X	X		

* These garments shall be made according to the body measurements in Table I (see page 250).

** An "X" in any colum indicates that the garment is to be made in that size.

Table V—Toddlers' Body Measurements
(Composite of boys' and girls' measurements)

MEASUREMENT	SIZE (number)			
	1	2*	3*	4*
Stature—inches	31	34	37	40
Weight—pounds (approx.)	25	29	34	38
GIRTH MEASUREMENTS †				
Chest	20	21	22	23
Waist	20	20½	21	21½
Vertical trunk	32½	34½	36½	39
Thigh	11½	12	12½	13
Neck Base	9⅝	10	10⅜	10¾
Armscye	8½§	9§	9½	10
Upper arm girth	5⅞	6⅛	6⅜	6⅝
WIDTH AND LENGTH MEASUREMENTS				
Cross-back width	8½	8⅝	9	9⅜
Shoulder length	2½§	2⅝	2¾	2⅞
Scye depth	3¾	4§	4¼	4½
Total crotch length	16	17	18	19
Shoulder and arm length	12½	13¾	15	16½
VERTICAL MEASUREMENTS ‡				
Head and neck length	6¼	6⅝	7	7¼
Cervicale height	24¾	27⅜	30	32¾
Cervicale to knee	17¼	18⅞	20½	22¼
Cervicale to waist, including curve of spine	8	8½	9	9½
Waist height	17	19¼	21½	23¾
Waist to knee	9½	10¾	12	13¼
Waist to hip	3⅜	3⅞	4⅜	4¾
Crotch height	11½	13⅛	14⅞	16⅝
Knee height	7½	8½	9½	10½
Ankle height	1⅝	1¾	1⅞	2⅛

* Body measurements for these sizes are identical with the corresponding sizes of the children's classification—Table 7 (see page 254).

† These measurements are *body*, not *garment*, measurements. The size-to-size gradations between these body measurements may be applied to garment patterns or specifications in grading, but they are not to be considered actual garment measurements.

‡ Since even gradations in vertical body measurements between sizes serve to make this standard more useful in grading garment patterns or specifications, minor adjustments (⅛ inch) have been made in a few instances to achieve this purpose.

§ Extrapolated.

Table VI—Grade Chart for Toddlers' Sizes

	GRADE BETWEEN 1-2	GRADE BETWEEN 2-3	GRADE BETWEEN 3-4
GIRTH MEASUREMENTS (inches)			
Chest	1	1	1
Waist	½	½	½
Vertical trunk	2	2	2½
Thigh	½	½	½
Neck base	⅜	⅜	⅜
Armscye	½	½	½
Upper arm girth	¼	¼	¼
WIDTH AND LENGTH MEASUREMENTS (inches)			
Cross-back width	½	⅜	⅜
Shoulder length	⅛	⅛	⅛
Scye depth	¼	¼	¼
Total crotch length	1	1	1
Shoulder and arm length	1¼	1¼	1½
VERTICAL MEASUREMENTS (inches)			
Head and neck length	⅜	⅜	¼
Cervicale height	2⅝	2⅝	2¾
Cervicale to knee	1⅝	1⅝	1¾
Cervicale to waist, including curve of spine	½	½	½
Waist height	2¼	2¼	2¼
Waist to knee	1¼	1¼	1¼
Waist to hip	½	½	⅜
Crotch height	1⅝	1¾	1¾
Knee height	1	1	1
Ankle height	⅛	⅛	¼

Table VII—Childrens' Body Measurements
(Composite of boys' and girls' measurements)

MEASUREMENTS	SIZE (number)					
	2	3	4	5	6	6X
Stature—inches	34	37	40	43	46	48
Weight—pounds (approx.)	29	34	38	44	49	54
GIRTH MEASUREMENTS *						
Chest	21	22	23	24	25	25½
Waist	20½	21	21½	22	22½	23
Hip	21½	22½	23½	24½	25½	26½
Vertical trunk	34½	36½	39	41	43	44½
Thigh	12	12½	13	13½	14	14½
Neck base	10	10⅜	10¾	11⅛	11½	11⅞
Armscye	9	9½	10	10½	11	11½
Upper arm girth	6⅛‡	6⅜	6⅝	6¾	7	7¼
WIDTH AND LENGTH MEASUREMENTS *						
Cross-back width	8⅝	9	9⅜	9¾	10⅛	10⅜
Shoulder length	2½	2¾	2⅞	3	3⅛	3⅛
Scye depth	4‡	4¼	4½	4¾	5	5⅛
Total crotch length	17	18	19	19¾	20½	21½
Shoulder and arm length	13¾	15	16½	18	19¼	20¼
VERTICAL MEASUREMENTS †						
Cervicale height	6⅝	7	7¼	7½	7¾	8
Cervical to knee	27⅜	30	32¾	35½	38¼	40
Head and neck length	18⅞	20½	22¼	24	25¾	27
Cervicale to waist, including curve of spine	8½	9	9½	10	10½	10¾
Waist height	19¼	21½	23¾	26	28	29½
Waist to knee	10¾	12	13¼	14½	15½	16½
Waist to hip	3⅞	4⅜	4¾	5⅛	5½	5¾
Crotch height	13⅛	14⅞	16⅝	18⅜	20⅛	21⅜
Knee height	8½	9½	10½	11	12	13
Ankle height	1¾	1⅞	2⅛	2⅜	2⅝	2⅝

* These measurements are *body*, not *garment*, measurements. The size-to-size gradations between these body measurements may be *applied* to garment patterns or specifications in grading but they are not to be considered actual garment measurements.

† Since even gradations in vertical body measurements between sizes serve to make this standard more useful in grading garment patterns or specifications, minor adjustments (⅛ inch) have been made in a few instances to achieve this purpose.

‡ Extrapolated.

Table VIII—Grade Chart for Childrens' Sizes

	GRADE BETWEEN 2-3	GRADE BETWEEN 3-4	GRADE BETWEEN 4-5	GRADE BETWEEN 5-6	GRADE BETWEEN 6-6X
		GIRTH MEASUREMENTS (inches)			
Chest	1	1	1	1	½
Waist	½	½	½	½	½
Hip	1	1	1	1	1
Vertical trunk	2	2½	2	2	1½
Thigh	½	½	½	½	½
Neck base	⅜	⅜	⅜	⅜	⅜
Armscye	½	½	½	½	½
Upper arm girth	¼	¼	⅛	¼	¼
		WIDTH AND LENGTH MEASUREMENTS (inches)			
Cross-back width	⅜	⅜	⅜	⅜	¼
Shoulder length	¼	⅛	⅛	⅛	0
Scye depth	¼	¼	¼	¼	⅛
Total crotch length	1	1	¾	¾	1
Shoulder and arm length	1¼	1½	1½	1¼	1
		VERTICAL MEASUREMENTS (inches)			
Head and neck length	⅜	¼	¼	¼	¼
Cervicale height	2⅝	2¾	2¾	2¾	1¾
Cervicale to knee	1⅝	1¾	1¾	1¾	1¼
Cervicale to waist, including curve of spine	½	½	½	½	¼
Waist height	2¼	2¼	2¼	2	1½
Waist to knee	1¼	1¼	1¼	1	1
Waist to hip	½	⅜	⅜	⅜	¼
Crotch height	1¾	1¾	1¾	1¾	1¼
Knee height	1	1	1	1	½
Ankle height	⅛	¼	¼	¼	0

Table IX—Slims—Girls' Body Measurements *

MEASUREMENT	SIZE					
	7S	8S	10S	12S	14S	16S
Stature	51	53	55	57½	60	60½
Weight (in pounds	53	59	67	77	89	103
GIRTH MEASUREMENTS						
Bust (chest)	24½	25½	27	28½	30	31½
Waist	20½	21	22	23	24	25
Hips	25¾	26¾	28¼	30¼	32¼	34¼
Vertical trunk	43½	45½	47½	50	52½	55
Neck base	11½	11¾	12¼	12¾	13¼	13¾
Armscye	11	11½	12	12¾	13½	14¼
Upper arm	6¾	7⅛	7½	7⅞	8⅜	8⅞
Elbow	7¾	8⅛	8½	8⅞	9⅜	9⅞
Thigh	14	14⅝	15½	16⅝	17¾	18⅞
Calf, maximum	9⅝	10	10½	11	11¾	12½
Knee, tibiale	10¼	10¾	11¼	11¾	12⅜	13
WIDTH AND LENGTH MEASUREMENTS						
Shoulder length	3⅜	3½	3⅝	3¾	3⅞	4
Cross-back width	10½	10¾	11¼	11¾	12¼	12¾
Cross-chest width	9	9¼	9¾	10¼	10¾	11¼
Crotch length, total	20¾	21½	22¾	24	25¼	26½
Total posterior arm length	17⅞	18¾	19⅝	20⅝	21⅝	22⅝
Shoulder and arm length	21¼	22¼	23¼	24⅜	25½	26⅝
VERTICAL MEASUREMENTS						
Head and neck length	8¼	8⅜	8½	8¾	9	9¼
Cervicale height	42¾	44⅝	46½	48¾	51	53¼
Cervicale to knee	28⅝	29⅞	31⅞	32⅝	34⅛	35⅝
Scye depth, along spine	5¼	5½	5¾	6	6⅜	6¾
Cervicale to waist, post.	11	11½	12	12½	13¼	14
Neck to waist, anter.	9⅞	10¼	10⅝	11	11⅝	12¼
Waist height	32	33⅝	35¼	37	38¾	40½
Waist to knee	17⅞	18⅞	19⅞	20⅞	21⅞	22⅞
Hip height	25¾	27	28¼	29⅝	31	32⅜
Waist to hips	6½	6⅝	6⅞	7¼	7⅝	8
Crotch height	23⅛	24¼	25⅜	26⅝	27⅞	29⅛
Knee height	14⅛	14¾	15⅜	16⅛	16⅞	17⅝
Ankle height	2½	2½	2⅝	2⅝	2⅝	2¾

Table X—Regulars—Girls' Body Measurements *

MEASUREMENTS	SIZE					
	7R	8R	10R	12R	14R	16R
Stature	51	53	55	57½	60	62½
Weight (in pounds)	60	66	74	84	96	110
GIRTH MEASUREMENTS						
Bust (chest)	26	27	28½	30	31½	33
Waist	22½	23	24	25	26	27
Hips	27½	28½	30	32	34	36
Vertical trunk	44½	46½	48½	51	53½	56
Neck base	11⅞	12⅛	12⅝	13⅛	13⅝	14⅛
Armscye	11½	12	12½	13¼	14	14¾
Upper arm	7⅜	7¾	8⅛	8½	9	9½
Elbow	8⅛	8½	8⅞	9¼	9¾	10¼
Thigh	15¾	16⅜	17¼	18⅜	19½	20⅝
Calf, maximum	10⅛	10½	11	11½	12¼	13
Knee, tibiale	10¾	11¼	11¾	12¼	12⅞	13½
WIDTH AND LENGTH MEASUREMENTS						
Shoulder length	3½	3⅝	3¾	3⅞	4	4⅛
Cross-back with	10¾	11	11½	12	12½	13
Cross-chest width	9⅜	9⅝	10⅛	10⅝	11⅛	11⅝
Crotch length, total	21½	22¼	23½	24¾	26	27¼
Total posterior arm length	18	18⅞	19¾	20¾	21¾	22¾
Shoulder and arm length	21½	22½	23½	24⅝	25¾	26⅞
VERTICAL MEASUREMENTS						
Head and neck length	8¼	8⅜	8½	8¾	9	9¼
Cervicale height	42¾	44⅝	46½	48¾	51	53¼
Cervicale to knee	28⅝	29⅞	31⅞	32⅝	34⅛	35⅝
Scye depth, along spine	5⅜	5⅝	5⅞	6⅛	6½	6⅞
Cervicale to waist, post.	11	11½	12	12½	13¼	14
Neck to waist, anter.	10	10⅜	10¾	11⅛	11¾	12⅜
Waist height	32	33⅝	35¼	37	38¾	40½
Waist to knee	17⅞	18⅞	19⅞	20⅞	21⅞	22⅞
Hip height	25¾	27	28¼	29⅝	31	32⅜
Waist to hips	6⅝	6¾	7	7⅜	7¾	8⅛
Crotch height	23⅛	24¼	25⅜	26⅝	27⅞	29⅛
Knee height	14⅛	14¾	15⅜	16⅛	16⅞	17⅝
Ankle height	2½	2½	2⅝	2⅝	2⅝	2¾

* The measurements are *body*, not *garment*, measurements. The size-to-size graduations between these body measurements may be applied to garment patterns or specifications in grading, but they are not to be considered actual garment measurements. All measurements except weight are expressed in inches. (One inch equals 2.54 centimeters; 1 pound equals 0.45 kilograms.)

Table XI—Chubbies—Girls' Body Measurements *

MEASUREMENTS	7½	8½	10½	12½	14½	16½**
			S I Z E			
Stature (in inches)	51	53	55	57½	60	62½
Weight	71	79	89	102	116	132
GIRTH MEASUREMENTS						
Bust (chest)	28½	29½	31	32½	34	35½
Waist	26	26½	27½	28½	29½	30½
Hips	30½	31½	33	35	37	39
Vertical trunk	46⅞	48⅞	50⅞	53⅜	55⅞	58⅜
Neck base	12½	12¾	13¼	13¾	14¼	14¾
Armscye	12¾	13¼	13¾	14½	15¼	16
Upper arm	8⅞	9¼	9⅝	10	10½	11
Elbow	8⅞	9¼	9⅝	10	10½	11
Thigh	18⅜	19	19⅞	21	22⅛	23¼
Calf, maximum	11¼	11⅝	12⅛	12⅝	13⅜	14⅛
Knee, tibiale	11¾	12¼	12¾	13⅜	14	14⅝
WIDTH AND LENGTH MEASUREMENTS						
Shoulder length	3⅝	3¾	3⅞	4	4⅛	4¼
Cross-back width	11¼	11½	12	12½	13	13½
Cross-chest width	10⅛	10⅜	10⅞	11⅜	11⅞	12⅜
Crotch length, total	23½	24¼	25½	26¾	28	29¼
Total posterior arm length	18¼	19⅛	20	21	22	23
Shoulder and arm length	21⅞	22⅞	23⅞	25	26⅛	27¼
VERTICAL MEASUREMENTS						
Head and neck length	8¼	8⅜	8½	8¾	9	9¼
Cervicale height	42¾	44⅝	46½	48¾	51	53¼
Cervicale to knee	28⅝	29⅞	31⅞	32⅝	34⅛	35⅝
Scye depth, along spine	5⅝	5⅞	6⅛	6⅜	6¾	7⅛
Cervicale to waist, post.	11	11½	12	12½	13¼	14
Neck to waist, anter.	10⅛	10½	10⅞	11¼	11⅞	12½
Waist height	32	33⅝	35¼	37	38¾	40½
Waist to knee	17⅞	18⅞	19⅞	20⅞	21⅞	22⅞
Hip height	25¾	27	28¼	29⅝	31	32⅜
Waist to hips	6⅞	7	7¼	7⅝	8	8⅜
Crotch height	23⅛	24¼	25⅜	26⅝	27⅞	29⅛
Knee height	14⅛	14¾	15⅜	16⅛	16⅞	17⅝
Ankle height	2½	2½	2⅝	2⅝	2⅝	3¾

* These measurements are *body*, not *garment*, measurements. The size-to-size gradations between these body measurements may be applied to garment patterns or specifications in grading, but they are not to be considered actual garment measurements. All measurements are expressed in inches. (One inch equals 2.540 centimeters; 1 pound equals 0.454 kilograms.)

** The 16½ measurements have been extrapolated.

Table XII—Grade Chart for Girls' Sizes

	GRADE BETWEEN 7-8	GRADE BETWEEN 8-10	GRADE BETWEEN 10-12	GRADE BETWEEN 12-14	GRADE BETWEEN 14-16
GIRTH MEASUREMENTS (inches)					
Bust	1	1½	1½	1½	1½
Waist	½	1	1	1	1
Hip	1	1½	2	2	2
Vertical trunk	2	2	2½	2½	2½
Neck base	¼	½	½	½	½
Armscye	½	½	¾	¾	¾
Upper arm	⅜	⅜	⅜	½	½
Elbow	⅜	⅜	⅜	½	½
Thigh	⅝	⅞	1⅛	1⅛	1⅛
Calf, maximum	⅜	½	½	¾	¾
Knee	½	½	½	⅝	⅝
WIDTH AND LENGTH MEASUREMENTS (inches)					
Shoulder length	⅛	⅛	⅛	⅛	⅛
Cross-back width	¼	½	½	½	......
Cross-chest width	¼	½	½	½	½
Crotch length, total	¾	1¼	1¼	1¼	1¼
Total posterior arm length	⅞	⅞	1	1	1
Shoulder and arm length	1	1	1⅛	1⅛	1⅛
VERTICAL MEASUREMENTS (inches)					
Head and neck	⅛	⅛	¼	¼	¼
Cervicale height	1⅞	1⅞	2¼	2¼	2¼
Cervicale to knee	1¼	2	¾	1½	1½
Scye depth, along spine	¼	¼	¼	⅜	⅝
Cervicale to waist, posterior	½	½	½	¾	¾
Neck to waist, anterior	⅜	⅜	⅜	⅝	⅝
Waist height	1⅝	1⅝	1¾	1¾	1¾
Waist to knee	1	1	1	1	1
Hip height	1¼	1¼	1⅜	1⅜	1⅜
Waist to hips	⅛	¼	⅜	⅜	⅜
Crotch height	1⅛	1⅛	1¼	1¼	1¼
Knee height	⅝	⅝	¾	¾	¾
Ankle height	0	⅛	0	0	⅛

Table XIII—Sub-Teen Girls' Body Measurements *

MEASUREMENT	SIZE				GRADE INCREASE FOR ALL SIZES
	8S	10S	12S	14S	
Stature (in inches)	58½	59½	60½	61½	
Weight	79	89	99	109	
GIRTH MEASUREMENTS *					
Bust	28½	30	31½	33	1½
Waist	23½	24½	25½	26½	1
Hip	30	32	34	36	2
Vertical trunk	52	53½	55	56½	1½
Thigh	16¾	18	19¼	20½	1¼
Neck base	12⅞	13¼	13⅝	14	⅜
Armscye	13	13½	14	14½	½
Upper arm	8	8½	9	9½	½
WIDTH AND LENGTH MEASUREMENTS *					
Cross-back width	11¾	12⅛	12½	12⅞	⅜
Shoulder and arm length	25¼	25¾	26¼	26¾	½
Shoulder length	3⅞	4	4⅛	4¼	⅛
Total crotch length	25	25¾	26½	27¼	¾
VERTICAL MEASUREMENTS **					
Head and neck length	8⅞	8⅞	8⅞	8⅞	0
Cervicale height	49⅝	50⅝	51⅝	52⅝	1
Cervicale to knee	33¼	34	34¾	35½	¾
Cervicale to waist, including curve of spine	13¼	13⅝	14	14⅜	⅜
Waist height	37	37⅝	38¼	38⅞	⅝
Waist to knee	20⅝	21	21⅜	21¾	⅜
Waist to hip	6⅞	7	7⅛	7¼	⅛
Crotch height	27	27⅜	27¾	28⅛	⅜
Knee height	16⅜	16⅝	16⅞	17⅛	¼

* These measurements are *body*, not *garment*, measurements. The size-to-size gradations between these body measurements may be applied to garment patterns or specifications in grading, but they are not to be considered actual garment measurements.

** Since even gradations in vertical body measurements between sizes serve to make this standard more useful in grading garment patterns or specifications, minor adjustments (⅛ of an inch) have been made in a few instances to achieve this purpose.

Suggested Sources of Inspiration

PERIODICALS

Women's Wear Daily
Vogue
Harper's Bazaar
Seventeen
Mademoiselle

Boucher, Francois. *20,0000 Years of Fashion*. New York: Abrams, 1967.
Contini, Mila. *Fashion: From Ancient Egypt to the Present Day*. New York: Odyssey, 1965.
Hill, Margot H., and Peter Bucknell. *The Evolution of Fashion*. New York: Reinhold, 1968.
Laver, James. *Children's Fashions in the 19th Century*. London: Batsford, 1951.
Moore, Doris. *The Child in Fashion*. London: Batsford, 1953.
Stavridi, Margaret. *History of Costume*. v. 1, The Nineteenth Century; v. 2, 1660–1800; v. 3, 1500–1660. Boston: Plays, Inc., 1968.
Tilke, Max. *Costume Patterns and Designs*. New York: Praeger, 1957.
——— *The Costumes of Eastern Europe*. New York: Weyhe, 1925.
Wilcox, Ruth Turner. *The Mode in Costume*. New York: Scribner, 1958.

MUSEUM FASHION COLLECTIONS

Fashion Institute of Technology, New York, N. Y.
Metropolitan Museum of Art, New York, N. Y.
Smithsonian Institute, Washington, D. C.
Arizona Costume Institute, Phoenix, Ariz.
Chicago Historical Society, Chicago, Ill.
Dallas Museum of Fashion, Dallas, Texas
Kansas City Museum of History and Science, Kansas City, Mo.
Los Angeles County Museum of Art, Los Angeles, Calif.

Bibliography

"Bonding." *American Fabrics Magazine*. Summer, 1965.

Borgenicht, Louis, as told to Harold Friedman. *The Happiest Man*. New York: G. P. Putnam & Sons, 1942.

Duval, Evelyn Mills. *Today's Teenagers*. New York: Associations Press, 1966.

1897 Sears Roebuck Catalogue. New York: Chelsea House Publishers, 1968.

Gesell, Arnold. *The First Five Years of Life—A Guide to the Study of the Pre-School Child*. New York: Harper & Row, Publishers, 1940.

Gesell, Arnold, Ilk, Frances and Ames, Louise Bates. *The Years from Ten to Sixteen*. New York: Harper & Brothers, 1956.

Joseph, Marjory L. *Introductory to Textile Science*. New York: Holt, Rinehart & Winston, Inc., 1966.

Josselyn, Irene M. *The Adolescent and His World*. New York: Family Service Association of America, 1952.

Linton, George E. *The Modern Textile Dictionary*. New York: Duell, Sloan & Pearce, 1963.

Man-made Fiber Fact Book. New York: Man-made Fiber Producers Association, Inc., 1967.

Mussen, Paul Henry; Conger, John Janeway, and Kagan, Jerome. *Child Development and Personality*. New York: Harper & Row, Publishers, 1963

Ryan, Mary Shaw. *Clothing, A Study in Human Behavior*. New York: Holt, Rinehart & Winston, 1966.

Schneider, Coleman. *Machine Made Embroidery*. Hackensack, N. J.: Schneider International Corp., 1968.

Smart, Mollie S. and Smart, Russel C. *Children, Developments and Relationships*. New York: The Macmillan Co., 1967.

Tate, Mildred Thurow and Glissen, Oris. *Family Clothing*. New York: John Wiley & Sons, 1961.

Textile Fibers and Their Properties. Greensboro, N. C.: Prepared by Burlington Industries, Inc., 1970.

Wingate, Isabel B. *Fairchild's Dictionary of Textiles*. New York: Fairchild Publications, Inc., 1967.

—— *Textile Fabrics and Their Selection*. Englewood Cliffs, N. J.: Prentice-Hall, Inc., 1970.

Index

Index

Index

Index